THE CREW OF RAINBOW'S END

*Adventures in
the Footsteps of
Captain Joseph Bates*

Linda Everhart

TEACH Services, Inc.
P U B L I S H I N G
www.TEACHServices.com • (800) 367-1844

World rights reserved. This book or any portion thereof may not be copied or reproduced in any form or manner whatever, except as provided by law, without the written permission of the publisher, except by a reviewer who may quote brief passages in a review.

The author assumes full responsibility for the accuracy of all facts and quotations as cited in this book. The opinions expressed in this book are the author's personal views and interpretations, and do not necessarily reflect those of the publisher.

This book is provided with the understanding that the publisher is not engaged in giving spiritual, legal, medical, or other professional advice. If authoritative advice is needed, the reader should seek the counsel of a competent professional.

Copyright © 2019 Linda Everhart
Copyright © 2019 TEACH Services, Inc.
ISBN-13: 978-1-4796-1140-9 (Paperback)
ISBN-13: 978-1-4796-1141-6 (ePub)
Library of Congress Control Number: 2019948541

Unless otherwise stated, all Bible text references are taken from the *Holy Bible*, New International Version®, NIV® Copyright © 1973, 1978, 1984, 2011 by Biblica, Inc.® Used by permission. All rights reserved worldwide.

Text references labeled (NLT) are taken from the *Holy Bible*, New Living Translation, Copyright © 1996, 2004, 2015 by Tyndale House Foundation. Used by permission of Tyndale House Publisher, Inc., Carol Stream, Illinois 60188. All rights reserved.

Text references labeled (MSG) are taken from *The Message*. Copyright © 1993, 2002, 2018 by Eugene H. Peterson.

Text references labeled (TLB) are taken from *The Living Bible* Copyright © by Tyndale House Foundation. Used by permission of Tyndale House Publishers Inc., Carol Stream, Illinois 60188. All rights reserved.

Many thanks to Lloyd and Dora Hallock, site managers of the Joseph Bates Home Museum, for their significant contributions to this book.

Published by

www.TEACHServices.com • (800) 367-1844

CHAPTER ONE

Breaking the uncomfortable silence, Gramps comments, "At least it's a sunny day with a light breeze."

"You're just trying to turn off my 'worry wart' button and it's not going to work! It's on high alert! Why did we consent for them to fly into this small local airport? Probably this airport doesn't even have their own fire truck for emergencies. I wouldn't be surprised if the pilot has to put the suitcases in the cargo hold himself, sell and collect the tickets, hand out pillows and the usual tasteless crackers and soda, plus make sure the passengers figure out which building to walk into when they deplane!" Gramma vehemently continues, "Do you think the children will be there already, just wandering around, worried about where we are, and if they're at the correct airport?"

"It's going to be OK, Gramma. The Lord is watching over them. Remember the scripture that says, 'He shall give His angels charge over you,' and, in *their* hands they shall bear you up"? After a prolonged thoughtful silence, Gramma replies, "This time it's probably going to have a very literal application." Gramps responds, "We're here now! I think I see their airplane coming in for a landing, good timing!"

Meanwhile, on the eight-passenger prop jet, there are only comments of hopeful expectations and future plans. Dave, the blond, slim built, oldest teenaged grandson, makes the pronouncement, "We should ask to go see the historic waterfront district on the way to the Bates' Home. It will save both time and gas, plus avoid having to go back there, later on. I have my cell phone charged and can take photos with that. Did you remember to get your camera, Sam?" After a period of nonresponse, Dave asks again, "Sam, did you get your camera?"

Sam, two years younger but the taller of the two teens is of dark complexion with curly black hair. He rolls his deep brown eyes upward,

and replies, "Yes, but why do you have to keep checking up on me? I'm old enough to take care of myself!"

Moving on to the diminutive youngest member of the family, Dave more softly asks, "What about you, Mae Lee, are you ready to get off? Do you have all your things ready to go?"

The seven-year-old Asian beauty of a sister, turns, smiles, showing her dimples, and replies, "I've been ready for hours, are we there now?"

Sam interjects in a mocking high voice, "Are we there now? Are we there now?"

Dave, interrupting the broken record says, "Yes, we are, you better let me go first and see if everything is okay."

With a look of hurt pride, Sam replies, "You don't think I can take care of myself? You are dead wrong there; I took care of myself for two years living on the streets! Don't you think I can walk from the plane to the terminal without your help?" After a heavy sigh from Dave, silence reigns until the pilot's voice is heard over the intercom, reminding the passengers to have their seat belts fastened, their trays in their upright position, and to please remain seated until further notice.

Exiting the plane first, Sam pauses to grab his suitcase from an attendant and then moves quickly off toward the main airport building. Dave gets both his and Mae Lee's suitcases, telling Mae Lee to stay close behind and hurries after Sam. When the two "brothers" meet, there is an exchange of words with both unhappy about the results, but they wait for Mae Lee to catch up, and then returning to their animated dialog continue their journey to find Gramma and Gramps. Once inside, the teens hurry into Gramma's welcoming arms. Gramps stands, looking around, and then asks an obvious question, "Where is Mae Lee?" With a gasp of disbelief that she's not with them, both boys turn, and run back in the direction they came, yelling "Mae Lee, where are you?" About in a panic, they tear through the "entrance" doors and out into the sunshine. Madly dashing here and there around tall containers and jumping over unclaimed luggage, they finally catch a glimpse of the missing girl, who is quietly breaking up her uneaten crackers and tossing them to the small sparrows at her feet. Both teens, panting

> *Madly dashing here and there around tall containers and jumping over unclaimed luggage, they finally catch a glimpse of the missing girl, who is quietly breaking up her uneaten crackers and tossing them to the small sparrows at her feet.*

from the race to find her, kneel with each giving her a sideways hug and affectionately messing her hair up in relief.

Mae Lee silently enjoying this unexpected show of affection, finally giggles, "Thank you, kind brothers, so happy to see you after so long apart."

Sam replies, "This is not funny, don't do that again!"

"Why didn't you follow us, Mae Lee? We were worried something awful when we couldn't find you!" adds Dave.

The still smiling girl just responds, "The birds needed some food—they were starving. I could tell because I know how it feels to be hungry, awfully hungry." Silently, this small group of travelers turns to find their grandparents once more.

With relief clearly written on her face, Gramma runs to give Mae Lee a long, welcoming embrace. Clearing his throat, Gramps greets them, "We are sooo glad you had a safe trip! It seems like a long time since we saw you last, but I guess, it has only been a couple of months."

Dave, a mature fifteen-year-old, taking on the role of spokesperson for the group, asks "Why do you have to be in Massachusetts so much of the time? We want you close so we can visit more often."

"Well, we have this opportunity to stay at the Joseph Bates Boyhood Home in the summer and fall to teach people about how God used Joseph to tell many others about Jesus and the Sabbath," responds Gramps.

Sam asks, "How did God use Captain Joseph Bates?"

"Yes, tell us the story, Gramps," adds Mae Lee.

Chuckling, Gramps returns, "The answer to that will have to wait a little while longer. I don't think I can drive and tell fascinating stories all at the same time!"

With the family together now, they find their car, store the luggage in the trunk, and stand outside the car awhile, discussing what to do during the grandchildren's visit to the grandparents' home on the grounds to the historic Adventist Joseph Bates Home. Dave suggests a trip to see the tall ships at the waterfront and all the reasons why to go there first. Gramps replies, "Occasionally, the tall ships do come into the New Bedford area, but there's none there now." Since the taller boy looks unhappy about this, Gramps asks, "What would you like to do, Sam?"

In response he blurts out, "I want to go sailing!"

Gramma, still refusing to let go of Mae Lee's hand, asks her, "What about you? What do you want to do?"

Quickly comes the joyous reply, "Let's go feed the seagulls!" After a group discussion and Gramma's promise of a scrumptious waiting supper, the group decides that they will go tomorrow to see the waterfront and have a sailing trip with feeding the birds included. All seem to agree to that plan and hurriedly get in the car and leave for their destination.

After a delicious meal and a group clean-up time, Gramps announces, "Okay, everyone into the living room—we have things to do, like planning for tomorrow's boating trip and discussing the long-range outlook for the ten days while you will be our treasured guests."

Gramma explains, "There are going to be many hours when Gramps and I will be committed to caring for the Bates' Home. We will be having visitors come from all over the world to see this Adventist Heritage Property and learn about the life of Captain Joseph Bates, and we need to give those tours."

Looking worried, Mae Lee asks, "Does that mean we can't be with you? Do we have to stay in this house all the time?"

"Of course not! I'm sorry that you thought that, Sweetie," Gramma softly answers. "However, there will be times when you'll be asked to stay in our home. We would never leave you alone on the property. If there is ever an occasion when we ask you to stay in the house, remember we literally are only a minute's run away. Moreover, if you have any problems or concerns, you can find us at the museum or taking care of the grounds. Matter of fact, your assistance in caring for the lawns, buildings, and flowerbeds are of extreme value to us. The exercise will give you strength, beauty of form, and dexterity!"

"I'll interpret that," interjects Gramps. "Kids, we just need your help. Is that, OK?" When he receives a nod from each, Gramps continues, "Gramma and I decided to give you each a different project to accomplish during your stay. We want you to have fun, but also to keep your learning skills going during the summer and not just become vegetables."

May Lee interrupts, "I no become a vegetable! Maybe … a tomato, but isn't that a fruit? I like tomatoes. Can we have tomato sandwiches tomorrow for lunch? I love tomato sandwiches with cheese and lettuce and mayonnaise."

Dave, holding a hand up to stop the deluge of food, orders, "Mae Lee, they're not talking about food. They just don't want our brains to rot and fall out our ears!"

Sam, looking closely at Dave's left ear cuts in, "Some people don't have anything left to lose if you ask me!"

Once the giggles and groans subside, Gramma explains the plan. "Each of you will receive two gifts, which are necessary to complete your assigned project." Moving to the front hall closet, Gramma returns quickly with three rather large, wrapped presents. "Why don't you open them one at a time, like we do at Christmas, just so everyone's attention is focused on what each is supposed to be accomplishing during your visit."

"Mae Lee, you go first since you're the youngest," suggests Gramps.

Mae Lee quickly responds, "Are you sure I'm the youngest?" Looking scornfully at her brothers. "Sometimes, I don't think so!" Seeing her brothers' facial expressions of "I'm going to get you later", Mae Lee says, "Okay, okay, I, the youngest, will go first."

The seven-year-old delicately removes the glorious pink bow and then starts to slowly peel the tape off, one piece at a time, so as not to tear the paper, which causes groans of despair from the waiting teenage males in the room. "Be patient brothers. Mae Lee will soon be done, not to worry!" she commands, causing increased levels of groans and rolling of eyeballs. Finally, as the paper is slowly unfurled from the top of the package, there erupt squeals of delight mixed with the bouncing of the shiny black-haired young girl. "I can't believe it! Oh, yes, finally my own bird!" as she pulls out a large plush toy seagull and hugs it tightly to her chest and face.

"Look deeper into the box," suggests Gramps. As Mae Lee lifts a book about seagulls, full of photos and interesting facts, she somberly starts to slowly read the first page ignoring everyone else in the room, but still hugging her "pet" bird.

"Is it time for my present, now?" questioned the thirteen-year-old ebony-skinned young man with eager anticipation.

"On with the show!" interjected Gramps, "This is fun!"

With a prolonged sigh, Gramma continues, "This gift is maybe not as dramatic, but I hope of interest to you, Sam, as it really is to me." At this pronouncement, a box, covered with antique looking designs, is handed to the gift recipient. Within less than a minute, the wrappings are discarded in shreds onto the floor and the box opened, revealing a telescoping spyglass (think binoculars for only one eye) and a book, decorated with pictures of the tall sailing ships of the 1800s, on the history of Buzzard Bay.

"Is this a book on buzzards or about ships?" Sam asks while leafing through it to see all the pictures.

Gramps suggests an answer, "Well, it is certainly about the exciting days of the tall ships' sailing sagas, however, Buzzard Bay refers to the large body of water that covers the entire area between Cape Cod, the New Bedford coastline, and the islands of Nantucket and Martha's Vineyard. According to history, the name Buzzard's Bay was most likely from people seeing turkey vultures or ospreys and thinking they were buzzards. Europeans settled Buzzards Bay in 1621. It is home to the National Marine Life Center, a marine animal hospital, and a science and education center dedicated to rehabilitating sea turtles, seals, dolphins, porpoises, and small whales, and to promoting scientific knowledge, and education in marine wildlife health, and conservation. So there's a lot to see. Matter of fact, look more closely in the bottom of your box, too."

Putting the spyglass down after staring at everyone in the room with it, Sam finally finds the item referred to by Gramps. "Tickets! Tickets to the New Bedford Whaling Museum? What's found there besides whales?" questions Sam.

"I think, you will be very pleased with what you find there." Gramma responds, "Now on to the last, but not least, of the presents. Here you go, Dave."

Dave takes the large, somewhat heavy rectangular box from his grandmother and stands holding it with hesitant speculation written all over his face, turning it over and feeling the contents move. Gramps cautions, "Careful, don't drop it!" With that statement, Dave looks all the more suspiciously at the gift. "And YOU thought I took too long getting at mine!" comments Mae Lee.

Sam adds, "On with it, now! Sir, make haste!" using a fake early American accent. Raising his hand to quiet the unruly crew, Dave takes on this last bastion of suspense and removes the covering quite adeptly. With *Ooos* and *Ahhs*, the three grandchildren are surprised to see a laptop notebook computer and a book entitled, *My Life and Adventures* by Joseph Bates.

Finally, having composed his thoughts enough to respond, Dave softly asks, "Why so expensive a gift for me? This is way more than the others received."

Gramps responds, "You were always concerned about others, sometimes to the neglect of yourself. You come rightly by it though, when your parents died in that car accident and you went to live with your aged grandparents, I remember how concerned they were about you needing a younger set of parents than themselves to give you proper care. With tears in their eyes, they made the arrangements for our son and wife to take you in and eventually adopt you. After that, you kept insisting that your adoptive parents take you to see your grandparents all the time, as much as time allowed them. You couldn't stand thinking about them being lonely in the nursing home. How we all mourned with you when they passed. It's been a rough road for you, as much as it has for your foster brother and sister. Each of you has had so much loss in your lives, but we hope to be there to help your second set of parents support and love you always. You are our God-given family that we cherish with all our hearts. OK, so I've got everyone crying now—sorry! I just had to say that to explain how special your visit is to us personally. This autumn, Dave, you'll be going away to a Christian boarding academy. You'll be needing a computer to do term papers and such, I guess, I think they still insist on torturing students with those kinds of things. I'm sure it's important for you … to do those papers … I think, … I'm just rambling on to keep from crying, myself."

"Yes, but we needed to have this discussion and many more like it," adds Gramma while wiping her and Mae Lee's tears away with tissues. "All these gifts are part of a puzzle that you get to put together. You along with Gramps and I will be working to compose a book. Mae Lee will be creating scrapbook pages to tell about the seagulls and other bird and plant life around Buzzard Bay. Sam will be writing and illustrating the significant secular history that occurred here, and Dave will be assigned to writing on the religious background and life of Captain Joseph Bates. When this book is put together, we want to make it available to other young people to help them learn three things: 1. How God created this beautiful aquifer and its wildlife; 2. How He raised up and guided this wonderful "land of the free and home of the brave" that we all share; 3. How God used Joseph Bates to prepare the Seventh-day Adventist Church to take the good news of the gospel into the entire world. Then Jesus will come to rescue those who love Him and, one day, restore this world to its original perfect condition. Ok, enough for tonight, it's getting late and we're all tired. I'll close with prayer and then on to bed!"

《 All these gifts are part of a puzzle that you get to put together. 》

"Dear Father, Lord, Savior, lover of our souls, thank you so much for the safety of the children as they traveled here. Thank you that we have the privilege to take care of the Joseph Bates Home and tell the story of his life and mission. Guide us in our decisions for tomorrow's plans. Watch over us and give each one a good night's rest. We ask this, please, in the precious name of our Friend, Jesus. Amen."

CHAPTER TWO

It was somewhere in the wee hours of the morning, not long after the new day began but before the first seagull even thought of stirring from its roosting spot, that muffled sobs came from the smallest bedroom in the house. Aroused by the sounds he knew so well, Sam stumbled sleepily from the room he shared with Dave. He knew with certainty the meaning behind the tears. Rubbing his eyes to see into the darkened bedchamber, he approached cautiously and sat on the edge of the small bed causing it to sag towards him. He is the first to speak, "Bad dream?"

Mae Lee, still softly sobbing, answers, "I didn't mean to wake you up."

"That's okay kid, I hear things in the night that others miss. It comes from growing up as a wild 'feral kid' … no one watching you, always taking care of yourself because your mom is high on drugs again, not aware of anything. I never knew who my dad was. Then one day, she didn't come home. Never did hear why. So, I just shoplifted food or clothes when I needed them or begged money from strangers just to stay alive. I figured which kinds of people I needed to stay away from to keep from getting hurt. Got so I could run pretty fast, knew which alleys went where, which fences I could climb that most people couldn't. You might have called me an ally cat." Then, turning to Mae Lee, he raises a hand to pet her hair, and emits a "Meow!"

In spite of her tears, Mae Lee chuckles softly and then returns to sobbing again, but this time into Sam's shoulder. "Why do I keep on seeing the explosion and the fear in my mother's eyes as she ran carrying me out of our burning house and into the jungle to hide me? Then she told me to stay there and be silent as she ran away to keep

the enemy from finding me. I never saw her again! Then I ended up in an orphanage. Sam, why?"

"Don't know kid," he replies, "but I think that someday we'll heal from all our horrid memories."

"You will, but maybe only to the extent of learning how to live without them crushing you. God can heal anything, but it takes time, at least that's what Dad and Mom say, anyways."

"Meanwhile, we're here to surround you with a loving family to walk with you through those sad memories and try to make happy ones to counteract the pain," says a new voice from the shadows cast by the nightlight. "Let's do a three-way hug, guys," suggests Dave.

Snuggling Mae Lee between them and messing her hair they cling together for a warm embrace. Mae Lee says softly, "I'm okay for now. Go to bed—we need our sleep to go sailing tomorrow, I mean today. Guess what I named my seagull? Bagel!"

"Great name, kid; couldn't have done better myself," replies Sam as he sets her down on her bed.

"A dignified name for one lowly seagull ... how cool is that! Sleep well, Mae Lee! We're not far away; come see us if you have any more scary dreams—good ones you can keep to yourself until after breakfast," commands Dave. Once all are back into their beds, Gramps and Gramma tiptoe back to their bedroom through the darkness. Once inside their room, a few tears are shed, but this time through warm smiles and a comforting embrace.

Sounds of bells, whistles, engines chugging on the nearby bay, plus the call of the seagulls claiming as theirs whatever tidbit that one of them found with the call of something like, "Mine, Mine, Mine!" ... the morning near Buzzard Bay has begun. When the day appears sunny and calm, Gramma and Gramps decide it is a good day to take the grandkids on a boat tour early, before the wind picks up. Soon a picnic lunch is prepared and all necessary boating paraphernalia stowed in the back of their four-door pickup truck—all this before a wakeup call is issued to the sleepyheads. However, not much call is needed today as excitement runs high for this boating adventure. The breakfast is soon consumed and cleanup dispatched with equal rapidity.

"Time to gather for morning worship," Gramps calls from the living room, "First one in gets to read the scripture!"

Sam, sliding in before the others, opens the Bible, and questions, "Where to Captain"?

"I want you to read Genesis 7:15–19," Gramps orders. "While you're finding that, I have a thinking question for everyone to be considering as the verses are read: What does this reading have anything to do with boats and our lives today? We'll have discussion and then prayer for the day, following."

"Okay, can do," replies Sam.

> *Pairs of all creatures that have the breath of life in them came to Noah and entered the ark. The animals going in were male and female of every living thing, as God had commanded Noah. Then the Lord shut him in. For forty days the flood kept coming on the earth, and as the waters increased they lifted the ark high above the earth. The waters rose and increased greatly on the earth, and the ark floated on the surface of the water. They rose greatly on the earth, and all the high mountains under the entire heavens were covered.*

"I know what it means!" Mae Lee joyfully answers. "God loves all the animals and we need to take some with us on your boat, today!"

"I agree with the first part, but our boat might be too small for the second part. What's say that we just take along your 'pet' seagull? I heard that you named it 'Bagel.' Is that because you like bagels?" asks Gramma.

"Well, it's like this Gramma—if my 'pet' was a gull from the sea, then it could be called a *seagull*, but Bagel is from Buzzard Bay, so it's a *baygull*. You get it Gramma?"

"Unfortunately, I do! That was a 'punish' joke if I ever heard one!" Gramma replies while hugging the little lass and her Bagel.

Changing the subject back to the original topic, Dave questions, "Gramps, what do you think those scriptures mean to us today?"

He explains, "To me, it means that because God knows the future and because He loves us, He arranges events to protect us from things we would never expect to happen. God knows how to protect His people! Also, I'd like to point out that our ship's name is Rainbow's End. Does that have anything to do with Noah's story?"

"Sure does," Sam replies. "After Noah and his family can leave their floating home, He gives them the sign of the rainbow as a promise that there will never be another world-wide flood. I think God didn't want them running back into the ark every time it rained. God cares about our worries, doesn't He?"

Gramps answers, "Yes, He is our forever Friend. Let's pray. Dear Father and Creator of the vast universe and all the tiny atoms that comprise it, we commit our care and the choices we make to You, today. May we hear Your still, small voice speaking clearly to our spiritual hearing. We want to think Your thoughts all day long. Thank You for hearing and answering our deepest needs. We love You and thank You for this beautiful day. Amen."

"We need to get moving now. I have checked the weather—always important when you are on the water. The forecast says we will have plenty of sun. That means we had better expect to wear sunscreen to keep from being sunburned. We will want to take jackets, too, because it can get cool in the evening. Now onto the marina!" exclaims Gramps.

"What is a marina?" Mae Lee wanted to know.

"Oh, that's where boats park," said Dave.

"You mean they park in the water? How do you keep the boat from floating away?" asked Sam.

"We tie it to a float buoy," said Gramps. "Is there a boy out in the water holding your boat?" Mae Lee questions.

"B-O-U-Y, not boy," corrects Gramps. "We'll show you how that works when we get to the boat."

"Oh, I can't wait!" exclaims Mae Lee.

Once all are snuggly packed into the truck, the stories continue to come along. "It looks like today should be a good beginner's day on the water," Gramps states the obvious. "We will take you sailing in the *Rainbow's End* and tell you about this harbor and the people who used to work here. We're just about to the harbor now. See those boats over there with the tall booms sticking up in the air? They are not sailing ships, but with their tall booms they might seem something like a tall sailing ship. Back before motors propelled boats, the wind was used to push boats along. This was called sailing. Ships could sail all over the world from this harbor."

"Gramps? If the wind is what made the ships go, why don't they just go the same direction as the wind?"

"Good question, Sam. We will try to show you more about how that works."

"Gramps, doesn't your boat have a motor?" Sam continues.

"Well, yes it does, but most of the time we just let the wind blow us along."

> *« We will take you sailing in the Rainbow's End and tell you about this harbor and the people who used to work here. »*

"I can't wait to see how that works," enthused Mae Lee. "I assure you that you will experience it and understand how, once you feel it," Gramps replies.

"Did you know that Joseph Bates sailed his ship out of this very harbor?" questions Gramma, as the car pulled up at the marina. Gramps opens the hatch and gives a bag to each to carry down to the dinghy dock.

"Who really was Joseph Bates, anyways?" asks Dave.

"Well, Joseph lived over 200 years ago and helped change his community and the face of religion in America and around the world," says Gramma.

"How did he do that, Gramma," asks Sam.

"Well, aren't you full of questions, you three. You will be here for a few days so you can save some of those questions for later on, okay?"

"Now follow Gramps," Gramma says. "He is headed to our dinghy named The Ark, which will take us out to our boat."

"What's a dinghy?" All the kids want to know.

Gramma replies, "It's a small boat to take us to our bigger boat."

"Oh, I see the dinghy! That really is a small boat! Do we have to ride in that?" asks Mae Lee.

"If you want to get to the sailboat, that's how you get there! For this number of people, we will have to make two trips in the dinghy. Who wants to go first?" asks Gramma.

"I do!" Dave and Sam say at the same time.

"Okay, when you step off the dock you need to bend low and step into the middle of the dinghy and grab the sides of the boat to steady yourself as you sit down. It is easy to lose your balance as the boat moves. Everyone settled?" asks Gramps.

"Yes," the boys answer.

"I'll be back for Gramma and Mae Lee soon," confirms Gramps. Then they leave for the bigger boat, anchored not far away. When they arrive at the sailboat, Gramps tells the boys how to scramble aboard and cautions them to be careful while he returned for Gramma and Mae Lee.

When they are finally all together on the sailboat, Gramps carefully ties the dinghy on behind and then sets about getting the boat ready to sail. He gives instructions to each of the kids for them to be constructively helping. Once the sails billow out and the pleasant summer breeze starts moving the boat through the water, all settle down in quiet amazement, each too absorbed in pleasant emotions to say anything. A rapture of delight fills each with wonder and peace. Something strangely addictive keeps luring them on to go farther and farther out to sea. Seagulls become their accompanying squadron, calling out to each other while looking for the possibility of a free lunch.

All of a sudden, Mae Lee realizes the opportunity that is now hers. "Gramma, did you remember food to feed the gulls?"

"I knew that if I didn't, you'd probably give our lunch away to them," replies Gramma. "Stay here, I'll get it." Several crusts of bread and old seed biscuits arrived with her return.

"How shall I get the food to them?" Mae Lee queries.

Gramps suggests, "Just toss the pieces, one at a time, as high as you can into the air. The gulls will do acrobatic stunts to make sure the food doesn't end up in the drink."

"Whose drink?" asks Mae Lee.

Dave replies, "The drink in this case is Buzzard Bay."

"Oh, I see, into the sea!" Mae Lee says as she throws the bird treats one by one into the air. "Come catch them!" she yells into the wind." With a vocal ruckus and skillful agility, Mae Lee's aerial friends perform loops and swirls to catch the leftovers in mid-air so that very few end up in the water, much to her wonder and delight. "Anymore, Gramma?"

"That's enough for now—we'll save some for later."

There is a seagull on that sailboat. "What is that bird"? asks Mae Lee.

"That is a cormorant and that other bird is a great black-backed gull," replies Gramma. "Get some paper and start a list of the birds that you can identify for your report. We have a bird book in the cabin. You can use that to identify more birds as we go along. Gramps, I have an idea, since it's almost noon, let's stop at this island and have a picnic lunch, and then go exploring," suggests Gramma.

"OK, take the tiller while I get the anchor ready to drop. We are in about fifteen feet of water so we can anchor right here," replies Gramps.

Soon the boat anchors and the dingy pulls alongside. Taking turns again, everyone is rowed to the large island. The walk along the path is pleasant. The bright blue sky, fluffy clouds, cool sea breeze, and the early summer flowers seem to be creating their own private garden. They place the picnic blanket and basket on a dry, mossy area and are about to start dinner when a thought crosses Mae Lee's mind. "Gramma, what kind of sandwiches did you bring?"

"I think there was someone who didn't think she could live much longer unless she could eat a lettuce, tomato, and cheese sandwich with mayonnaise on it, was that you?" replies Gramma. With a squeal of joy and a hug for the cook, Mae Lee offers to say the blessing as soon as possible. With several hungry sailors present, lunch seems to go by fast.

"Look everyone—there is a herring gull and there is another one, Mae Lee."

"What is beside that gull?" queries Mae Lee.

"Oh, it is a downy baby. How cute!" replies Gramma. The next half hour or so is spent watching seagulls, finding nests, eggs, and enjoying a wonderful summer day at a secluded seagull rookery. Sam had remembered to bring his camera along so that Mae Lee would have pictures for her report. All too soon, Gramps reminds everyone that they should get back to the sailboat and head to the mooring.

As each one takes turns running the tiller—the part that steers the boat—they find it to be harder than Gramps made it look. Thankfully they are in a large bay with room to learn without running aground or hitting rocks. "We're going to tack the boat around and head over toward the historical area of this bay," suggests Gramma. "Boats are a big part of life here. Fairhaven especially was one of the busiest ports in America. There's lots of other history here too. On our way home, we will pass some very old homes—some belonged to famous people in our country's history. Several United States presidents were from Massachusetts. Four hundred years ago, Native Americans, called Indians by the original Europeans explorers, who thought that they had arrived in the East Indies, inhabited this area. They hunted wild animals, caught fish, and gathered nuts and berries to use for food. They had simple dwellings made from tree bark and young tree poles. The first white settlers came here looking for land to cultivate and a place to live free from religious persecution. Sadly, some of the very people who wanted to be free to worship God only wanted to allow their own way of worship.

"Some of the first settlers in Fairhaven came here because their ideas were not welcome in the first settlements in Plymouth and Boston. John Cooke came over from England on the Mayflower sailing ship at the age of fourteen. After living in Plymouth for forty years, he chose to move because his style of worship was not welcome in Plymouth. Most of the Indians were friendly to the new settlers, but when they were cheated and driven away from their lands, some became angry and destroyed the European settlements. What is now called Fairhaven was destroyed during King Phillip's War of 1775. King Philip was an Indian chief and wanted to help his people get their lands back from the settlers. On our way home, we will drive by a seaport harbor on the Acushnet River. Today, many commercial fishing boats and pleasure boats call this harbor their home. From here, ships can go to all parts of the world; so it is considered a gateway to the ocean."

That evening after a tasty meal and showers, it is time for worship. Gramps asks what was their favorite part of the day. Each has a different response. Sam is surprised and happy that there was cell phone coverage from the boat. That raises the question of how that could be important. They decide that the phone could be used to get updated weather reports, to request help in emergencies, to notify others when they were delayed, and to talk with the marinas. Then Gramps shows them the navigation program that is available on both his iPhone® and iPad®. It gives water depth, location of obstructions, shoreline, tide direction and speed. Gramps comments, "As important as all these digital devices are, there is even a more accurate source of information needed to guide us in our own personal voyages. Mae Lee, would you please get the Bible and find, Isaiah 30:21?"

"OK, Gramps, if you will help find where that is," responds Mae Lee.

After studying the verse over a little, Mae Lee begins, "Whether you turn to the right or to the left, your ears will hear a voice behind you, saying, 'This is the way; walk in it'."

"Wow, that's a real special promise, Gramps, but who is the 'him' that the verse talks about?"

Gramps replies, "Earlier in that chapter it tells who 'him' is. Read verse 18."

"Yes, this does, I understand it now, Gramps," adds Mae Lee. "Yet the LORD longs to be gracious to you; therefore He will rise up to show you compassion. For the LORD is a God of justice. Blessed are all who wait for Him!"

"To illustrate this, I have a story from the life of Captain Joseph Bates. Settle back and relax a little, then we'll have prayer, and off to bed," Gramps suggests. There is a round of favorable comments, like "Yes, finally!" "Whoopee!" "Why not more than one?" Gramps defends himself with, "Okay, I know we've been slow in getting to this, but you must admit, we've been very busy."

"The story takes place in the fall of 1847 when Captain Bates was already an experienced preacher and was trying to share the Biblical understanding of the seventh-day Sabbath to people who didn't understand it yet. This day, he sat at home and started to write a book of about 100 pages to explain its importance. His problem was that he had spent so much of his money on preaching trips and writing other books, that he didn't have enough to print this one. He had only a York shilling, which was worth about twelve-and-a-half cents. Don't worry about the half-cent now; just trust me that it wasn't worth much. You see Bates had gone from having several thousands of dollars in 1844 to a state of poverty because of his giving so much to share the news of Christ's soon coming. Therefore, even though he didn't have the money to publish it, by faith that God would supply all his needs, he began writing the book.

"Just then, his wife Prudence walks in and says she needs some flour to make bread. He asks her, 'How much?' and she replies, 'About four pounds.' He walks to the store to buy it. When he gets there, he finds out that the price of the flour takes all his money, however, he still buys it, walks back home, and then gives it to his wife. She is dumbfounded! 'You only got this much flour!' She was expecting something like a barrel of flour. When he explains that he couldn't afford anymore because now all their money was gone, Prudence asks, 'What are we going to do?' Bates replies, 'I am going to write a book; I am going to circulate it, and spread this Sabbath truth before the world.' To that his wife has another question, 'What are we going to live on?' To this Bates replies, 'The Lord is going to open the way.' She replies, 'That's what you always say,' bursts into tears, and runs to her bedroom to cry. Bates just quietly sits down and keeps writing because he couldn't think of anything else to do. About a half hour later, he sensed a still small voice directing him to go to the post office, which he did. He found that there was an envelope for him, but the postage was due and he didn't have the money to pay it! He suggested that the postman open the letter because he had been impressed that there was money in it. There was a $10 bill, which was really a lot of money back then. With it, he paid the postage, went to the store, and bought a barrel of flour, potatoes, sugar, and other necessary items and had them delivered to his front porch. He cautioned the delivery boy that the lady of the house would object because she wouldn't have enough money to pay for it. He was to leave it there anyways. Bates didn't go directly home. He went and made arrangements to have his book published now that he had some of the money he needed to pay for it. When he got home, his wife met him at the door, complaining about the food that was delivered against her will. He explained the whole story to her after which she went back into her room to have another cry, but this time a cry of happiness for the Lord's miraculously providing for their needs."

"So how does this story illustrate the Bible verse?" Gramps questions.

Dave responds, "God doesn't need digital devices to speak to us and His ways are always best."

"Dave, would you please have prayer thanking the Lord for that promise?"

"Sure. Dear God, we know that all things are possible with You. Help us to trust You, because Your love for us is like sunshine on a stormy day. We thank You for Your care and all the wonderful things we've seen and done today. Please watch over us as we sleep and give everyone a good night's rest. Also, watch over Mom and Dad on their mission trip and may many come to know You through their ministry. Amen"

"Amen. Amen—thanks Dave, off to bed now everyone, sweet dreams, see you in the morning," replies Gramps.

"What about a five-way hug?" requests Gramma.

After the embrace was over, Mae Lee asks, "How did you know that we do group hugs?" With twinkles in their eyes, Gramps and Gramma just shoo them off without answering.

CHAPTER THREE

A THICK, COOL fog had silently rolled in from the water's edge, surrounding the weary sailors' sleeping quarters during the night. The damp morning's dawn goes unnoticed much longer than usual because weary bodies thought they needed more rest to recover from yesterday's journey. Finally, the seagull's incessant vocalizations break through the sweet dreams of the smallest resident at the Joseph Bates' Home. Mae Lee's eyes light upon her mascot companion. They are nose to beak, so to speak, with all eyes open now. "Come with me, Bagel, we'll get everyone breakfast! What shall we have for a surprise meal? I wonder if there are any tomatoes left to make sandwiches. I won't try to use the stove; so it should be okay. Let's go!" Bagel doesn't reply, but is carried along with the enthusiasm of the plan. Silently, bare toes tread lightly over the hallway and stairs to the silent kitchen below.

After several almost ripe tomatoes are located, the plan begins to unfold before these early morning conspirators. Because mayonnaise and cheese are no longer available, mustard and butter are substituted. Pressing farther into the depths of the refrigerator, Mae Lee finds jars of various sizes that smelled pleasant. "These might be a good to add," thinks Mae Lee. "Now, where is the lettuce?" Something that resembles a green, leafy vegetable will have to do. With much careful cutting, carving, and spreading, Mae Lee happily finishes her masterpieces of culinary art before the first morning straggler arrives for breakfast. She only has time to put out dishes and some tumblers for juice to surprise the family as they groggily arrive. With a little gasp, Gramma is the first to find the surprise banquet, followed soon after by the rest of the crew. "Surprise! Breakfast is all ready! Just be seated, I'll get the juice soon," announces the little chef. Though silent, Bagel is still counted as an accomplice to this most unusual "bon appetite." Warily, each silently took a seat and began to partake of this original creation. Bulging eyes and chocking coughs are somewhat held in check so as not to crush the joy in the little girl's eyes.

At last, Gramps finds his voice, and, clearing his throat, asks, "Please tell me the ingredients of this surprising breakfast of delight?"

"Oh, I'm so glad you like it, Gramps. I'm really not sure of everything in it because I couldn't read all the labels. I just know it's good for you. It will keep you going all day," answers Mae Lee.

"You're right on that one, little miss; you get lots of things moving with this, I'm sure," returns Gramps. Gramma, coming up with a face-saving idea, asks Mae Lee to please go get dressed with some more clothes on so that she won't catch cold. By the time Mae Lee arrives back, the "sandwiches" are not to be found.

When Mae Lee expresses dismay that she didn't get to taste her sandwich, Sam responds, "Guess I got too hungry and just couldn't stop eating. I'll make you one myself—how's that grab ya? Chef Par Excellence is ready to serve you!" laughs Sam.

After a prolonged silence, Mae Lee's eyes begin to fill with tears that drip over her quivering lips, "You don't make up stories too well, Sam. I can tell that you didn't eat my sandwich."

As Mae Lee turns to run away, Gramma, kneels beside her to hug her and Bagel, "We were charmed by your desire to please us with the gift of a feast. Not all creations come out right the first time. I remember one of the first meals I cooked for Gramps and his parents ... well, let's just say we had a good laugh over it and threw much of it away. Even though we didn't think the sandwiches were the best for our breakfast, I've saved the discarded remains to feed the seagulls. What do you and Bagel think about that?"

"Can we eat first? I'm so hungry!" answers Mae Lee.

Dave laughs, "I think we all are! You and I will work together to make my scrumptious oatmeal, raisin cooked cereal delight. Want to learn how?"

Rubbing her wet cheeks dry, Mae Lee responds, "Thank you, Dave, I'd like that."

Sam, assuming a mock upset pose, observes, "You like his food better than mine? I understand that Dave is considered a 'cereal killer' in these parts."

Gramps cautions, "No puns only raisin buns for breakfast! Let's get moving before we all perish! Then let's meet in the living room for worship."

With the meal complete and clean-up accomplished, all gather to read God's Word together and pray. Gramps requests, "Gramma, would you find Acts 10:34–35 and read it to us, please?"

"Yes, here it is. 'Then Peter began to speak: "I now realize how true it is that God does not show favoritism but accepts from every nation the one who fears him and does what is right."'"

Gramps continues, "I have a story about Joseph Bates for you that shows how he valued each person he met, regardless of what others thought of that person. In other words, he tried to imitate God by not showing favoritism because of what a person looked like or how they behaved. After Bates became a follower of our Lord Jesus, he also became a preacher of the good news of Jesus' love and His soon coming to anyone who would listen. He paid his own expenses to travel sometimes by train, horse and carriage, or walking many miles. One of the places he went, at the risk of his life, was to the southern part of United States. It was dangerous for him because he was an abolitionist, which meant that he was against treating people as slaves. In the south, at that time, many people were made to work hard with no pay and kept almost like animals with no rights of their own. These people were called slaves. Bates bravely went preaching there, even though he was opposed by the slave owners. They accused him of trying to free their slaves, to which he responded that he was trying to free the slaves and them, too, from sin so that they would be ready for Jesus to come and take them all to heaven. This got them mad and they threatened to ride him out of town on a rail, to which Bates replied, 'We are ready for that, sir. If you put a saddle on it, we would rather ride than walk … You must not think that we have come six hundred miles through the ice and snow, at our own expense, to give you the Midnight Cry, without first setting down and counting the cost. And now, if the Lord has no more for us to do, we had lief [gladly] lie at the bottom of the Chesapeake Bay as anywhere else until the Lord comes. But if he has any more work for us to do, you can't touch us!' The slave owners were so taken back by his statements that they didn't try to hurt him. I'm sure God placed His protecting

> *We help ourselves and others by being an example of Jesus even when it is scary to do that.* 〉

hand over him, too. Joseph's words, faith, and example are for us to copy even today. We help ourselves and others by being an example of Jesus even when it is scary to do that. Let's pray. Creator of all things, great and small, thank You that You are Lord of all. Please help us to be tools in Your hands to demonstrate Your love to someone, today. Watch over each one and give us words to share Your grace in everything we say."

"Gramps, that was almost a poem!" observes Sam.

"I always thought I might be a poet because my feet are *Longfellows*," Gramps replies and then looks confused that no one seems to appreciate his implied pun.

Gramma sighs and says, "I'll explain it later, kids. Let's just get on with our plans for the day. We need everyone to help with caring for the lawns, flowerbeds, and cleaning the buildings, which includes this house, the carriage house (now called the Welcome Center), and the Joseph Bates' Home. Everyone please start by making beds, straightening up your room, decide which clothes to wear for Sabbath tomorrow, and then report back here for a list of more chores that need doing. Now be gone, with a song, all day long!" When all stop to look quizzically at her, Gramma responds, "My feet are *Longfellows*, too, I guess." Giggling, the kid crew goes into action.

After the house cleaning chores were done and the dew gone from the grass, the crew moves onto lawn and garden care. While Gramps drives the riding mower, the boys take up the task of raking and removing unwanted brush and branches. Mae Lee follows Gramma to the gardens to weed, cultivate, and contemplate what new plantings or arrangements should be done. Because the gardeners are so involved in their tasks, they are unaware of an elderly lady approaching them from an adjoining lawn until she speaks, "Well, well, well, what do we have here, a little Chinese doll? Where did you get her? And those too upstart teens, what about them?"

"Oh, good morning Miss Mabel, how are you today?" Gramma apprehensively replies.

"Better not to talk about that ... don't want to ruin your morning with complaints," she replies. Pointing to the three youngsters she continues,

"Just want to make sure you point out to them where my property lines are because I don't want to see them over here. No telling what havoc they might do. Couple of them are foreign, aren't they? Don't think I would trust them with my yard work and gardens! Neighbor, you better be careful with them running around loose. Got to get back inside, rheumatism acting up. Remember what I said!" With that farewell statement, Miss Mabel hobbles back home.

Finally, when Mae Lee feels that it is safe to speak, she asks, "Gramma, what did we do wrong that she doesn't trust us?"

Hugging the girl, Gramma replies, "You and your brothers did nothing to deserve her complaints. It's this way, you see, some people have so much poison inside of them that they can't help spilling some of it on others, every so often."

"How do 'they' get that poison in them and carry it around without them dying," Mae Lee wonders.

Gramma returns, "That's it, Mae Lee. Inside they do die a little each day."

"Is there anything we can do to help get the poison out of her?" Mae Lee persists.

"Only love is stronger than hate," Gramma says while watching the elderly neighbor walk slowly up her rickety steps and into the backdoor. "Let's pray for her right now," Gramma suggests. "Dear Lord, we thank You for Your love and forgiveness to us even when we make mistakes. We pray that You give us a forgiving spirit like Yours and find some way to show Your love to Miss Mabel, today. Amen. Okay, I think that after we pick some tomatoes, onions, and lettuce from the vegetable garden by the house, we're done with gardening."

"Gramma, I've got an idea. It looks like you have lots of tomatoes; could I give some to our poisoned neighbor?" queries Mae Lee.

Laughing, Gramma hugs Mae Lee again and replies, "Why, yes, that might be just the antidote she needs. You'd better not go alone, just in case."

"Just in case of what, Gramma?" Mae Lee returns.

"Not to worry, everything will be okay … sorry I said that. Let's just get going," Gramma ends the conversation.

With the vegetables secured and moved into the clean kitchen, Gramma puts some of the tomatoes in a paper bag and leaves them by the door. She says, "Mae Lee, why don't you go out and see how your brothers are doing, I'll be busy here for a while."

The girl finds her Bagel and starts to the door. When she sees the sack of tomatoes, she picks them up and takes them with her. Seeing that Dave and Sam appear to be finished, she walks over to tell them of the conversation with Miss Mabel. "Gramma is right, all we can do is show her kindness. Then maybe, she'll come to trust us," Dave suggests.

"I could offer to do some of her yard work, get the hanging branch out of the tree in her backyard, or fix those falling-down stairs," ventures Sam.

"You'd better not try doing anything with those stairs by yourself," Dave states.

"There you go questioning what I can do again without giving me a chance to try," Sam says sharply.

After a time of silence, Sam replies, "Sorry, Dave, if you need help, Gramps or maybe I could help in that project."

《 *Stay away from my porch. I gave orders for you all not to come on my lawn. How dare you?* 》

Mae Lee interjects, "Gramma said that I shouldn't go alone to Miss Mabel's house to give her these tomatoes. Why don't you two go with me?"

"Sure, let's all go. You should be safe with two male bodyguards," laughs Dave.

As the three pick their way over brambles towards the spinster's back-door, Miss Mabel is watching them behind lace curtains with first concern and then anger growing up inside of her. She hobbles to the door to meet them before they could even climb her steps, pushes open the door part way, and sternly orders, "Stay away from my porch. I gave orders for you all not to come on my lawn. How dare you?"

Frozen in mid-step by the outburst, Dave replies, "We only came to give you some of Gramma's fresh tomatoes from the garden and offer to clean up your yard. Sorry, we upset you."

Taken back by this reply, Miss Mabel's interest moves to the sack in Mae Lee's hand, "You say they are fresh picked tomatoes? And you're willing to take on my back lawn for free?"

Sam answers, "We wouldn't think of doing it any other way because we're neighbors and that's what neighbors are for, so our mom and dad always say. Also, I could get that big limb down that's hanging over your backyard if that's okay with you."

At this Miss Mabel silently looks them over from head to toe, and asks, "You three don't have the same parents? How did that happen?"

Mae Lee answers while handing the sack of tomatoes over to the questioner, "Dave is adopted and Sam and I, Mae Lee, are foster children until the adoption papers come through, but we're all part of the same family. Our dad is the son of your neighbors. So that makes them our Gramma and Gramps."

"Well, I guess if you're related, so to speak, to the docents at Joseph Bates' Museum, you're probably trustworthy. Okay, go ahead, give it a try, and see what you can do. Be careful, if you get hurt, I'm not responsible for it, you understand!" Miss Mabel ends the conversation and slowly shuts the door and moves to the window facing the back yard so she can watch them through the dusty drapes.

"Just how are you planning to get that tree limb down? Have you ever done anything like that before? Maybe we should ask Gramps," Dave states emphatically.

"It's okay, I've got a plan. I'll get the large rope I saw in the woodshed, climb the tree, tie it around the broken limb, and then we'll just pull the rope from a safe distance away. No, I haven't done it before, but I've done a lot of climbing. No sense getting Gramps … he's busy preparing the museum for a group visiting tomorrow. I could probably do it all by myself, but I might need help in pulling the rope hard enough to make the limb fall. I'll go get the rope, be right back," Sam calls over his shoulder as he runs towards the woodshed. Once back, Sam carries the rope slung over his left shoulder as he makes quick work of scrambling up the tree. After tying the rope on the limb, Sam carefully plans and executes a series of loops and knots. Then he drops the remainder of the rope, and it uncoils as it falls to the ground. The teens had made sure that Mae Lee was near the museum and made her promise not to move until the branch was down. Pulling together, the fellas get the dead branch rocking. After much exertion and a few rope burns on their hands, the branch crashes down near the base of the tree. A loud cheer erupts, not only from Mae Lee and the teens, but also from Miss Mabel who by then was standing on the rickety back porch steps.

"Well done, well done, you did it, didn't think you could. How did you learn to tie knots like that?" asks their excited elderly spectator.

"Well, when I lived on the streets by myself, there was this older homeless man, Jason, who lived in the neighborhood. To pass the time, he taught me a lot about knots. You know homeless people move a lot … don't know where he went. One day, he was just gone! I missed him; he was a friend when I really needed one," explains Sam. There is a long, quiet pause as a few tears slowly dripped from Sam's eyes and, surprisingly enough, from Miss Mabel's eyes, too. The silence is broken by Gramma calling the grandkids to come eat.

"We'll come back after dinner and take the brush away, Miss Mabel," states Dave. "See you then."

The older woman stands silently watching them leave, and then slowly returns to her home, pausing in thought looking back at the fleeing young people.

CHAPTER FOUR

DURING DINNER, A lively discussion takes place on the plans for the evening and the coming Sabbath day. Gramma suggests that a pleasant evening walk along the bay area near a certain important bridge (that no longer exists) would be just the thing to do to welcome the day of rest. Also, she describes the need to soon distribute the uneaten breakfast remains to the hungry seagulls that live in that area. Gramps agrees by commenting, "That would kill two birds with one stone, to quote a famous saying."

Mae Lee stops chewing, swallows hard, and retorts, "It is not right to kill birds with stones!"

"No, that's not what Gramps means," adds Dave. "It's just an old saying that means to do two different tasks at the same time with one action. No birds will be harmed in the process."

"Guess I need to be more careful about what I quote," apologizes Gramps. "Sorry, I didn't mean to sound mean. Oh, by the way, I wanted to tell you a little more about the poet, Henry Wadsworth Longfellow, since I referred to him this morning."

Sam interjects, "I thought you were just describing your shoe size!"

After the laughing spell subsides, Gramps says, "Okay, on with a quote I intended to recite, 'My soul is full of longing for the secret of the sea, and the heart of the great ocean sends a thrilling pulse through me.'"

Continuing, Gramps raises a question, "When can we go sailing again? I figure that we could fit in two more times before the kid's departure date arrives." A short happy/sad silence settles in as each contemplates a response.

"I love sailing, but don't want to think about my grandchildren leaving," answers Gramma, "What about Monday and then the last day before everyone leaves?"

"This is a little like sweet and sour sauce," comments Mae Lee sadly.

Gramps tries to change the mood of the family by suggesting a pleasant plan, "What's say we sail Monday and then again on Thursday? That will give our student authors three days to complete their projects. To help them gather information, we need to also set a date to visit the Whaling Museum and Mystic Harbor."

"I think I can find a substitute docent for the museum for Sunday and Monday; and then Thursday is our day off anyways. That should work. Everybody happy with those plans?" asks Gramma.

After all give a silent nod, Sam adds, "I'll be happy to see Mom and Dad again, but not happy about leaving here."

"Me too," adds Mae Lee and Dave.

"On Sabbath, we need to host a visiting group from an Asian country on tour of the Adventist Heritage Sites in the United States. They will be arriving sometime late morning, tomorrow. What that means is that we will have a Sabbath School in our home after breakfast, and then a type of church service in the carriage house with our visitors when they arrive," announces Gramps. This announcement is followed by clapping and cheers.

"Finally, we get to hear a full tour of the Bates Home and more stories about Joseph Bates' life. That should sure be interesting and help me with my project," Dave joyfully adds.

"Okay, lets finish up dinner, and get on with the show!" Gramma enthusiastically finishes the discussion.

"Oh, we forgot to tell you that we need to go back over to Miss Mabel's house because we promised to clean up the brush and fallen limb in her back yard after we ate," states Sam, "It shouldn't take us long, right, Dave? Then we'll be right back."

Gramps, looking a little surprised, questions, "When did that limb fall down? I was planning on trying to do something about it, but wasn't quite sure how I'd do it."

"Sam climbed the tree with your rope, tied some really well-placed knots around it, and then we pulled the other end of the rope until it fell down. No problem," answers Dave.

Mae Lee adds, "We took the tomatoes over to her, too. Like you said, Gramma, I didn't go alone. We'll help with the kitchen first."

Gramma and Gramps exchange questioning looks and then Gramps suggests, "Before you ever attempt another trapeze exhibition, please tell me so I can bring a camera or at least have my phone handy to call 911. I wish you would have asked me first, okay?"

Sam replies, "Sorry, Gramps, I just didn't want to bother you because I knew you were busy with the museum."

"You're more important to me than having a neat lawn, Sam. Accidents happen to even experienced tree surgeons. So please, no climbing unless, I give the okay," Gramps finishes.

When the meal and cleanup are completed, the group gathers all that they need for the excursion to feed the gulls. Gramma gets the leftover breakfast and something to wash hands with afterwards. "I'll get my camera," plans Sam, "I don't want to miss a good photo-op of Bagel's friends coming to dine."

"Oh, yes, I almost forgot my fuzzy friend," Mae Lee says as she runs to get her toy.

Gramps explains the hike's itinerary. "We will be going to a bridge site that is important to the story of Bates. The bridge once connected New Bedford and Fairhaven over the Acushnet River. It is no longer there, but a big moment in the history of the Sabbath happened there. Let's get going. I hope that after we deliver the seagull's take out order, we can watch the sun slide down near the horizon and reflect off the bay with the Sabbath hours soon to begin. I'll tell you the whole story about that historic spot for vespers this evening after we return."

The early evening air is pleasant, filled with the rasping call of seagulls. Arriving, the grandkids are a little disappointed as to a lack of park benches, but they are on a mission to feed Mae Lee's feathered friends. So no one complains. Once the gulls see the group's intent, a ruckus breaks out as to which bird can get the most. They even fight over the un-ripened slices of tomato covered with mustard thrown up into the air. The laughs and cheers of the distributors of the undesired breakfast foods fill the air. All too soon, it seems, the food is consumed. The family waits a while to see if an artist's sunset seascape would start to appear in the western sky. Knowing that it would be best to arrive home while there is sufficient sunlight to be safe, the group ambles towards the museum, occasionally glancing towards the glowing oranges and pinks of the sunset as it filled the horizon.

Arriving back at the grandparent's home, Gramma suggests, "Why doesn't everybody get on their pajamas and come back down for an evening of sitting around the fireplace for a hot drink and peanut butter and jam sandwiches? Gramps, would you please start a small fire in the fireplace, too? Soon there will be a little chill to the air once the sun goes down and the cooling bay mist creeps in."

"I love to build fires in the fireplace. How about you guys, you want to learn how to do that?" asks Gramps. With a unanimous positive vote, the prospect of a very pleasant evening vespers begins. Sam and Dave go with Gramps to the woodshed for kindling and small logs for the fireplace, while Mae Lee stays with Gramma to get the light supper together. When they had just gotten the fire going and the food lined up on a small table, the doorbell rings, startling them all. Gramma starts for the door accompanied by Mae Lee. Much to their astonishment, there stands Miss Mabel looking quite uneasy about something.

Gramma is the first to find words to say, "Miss Mabel, come in and have a seat by our fireplace, there's always room for more. We're glad you came because we'd like you to share our simple evening refreshments and join our story time."

"Yes, I mean no, I didn't mean to intrude on your family gathering. I just had to say something to you all so that I could sleep tonight with a clear conscience." After a pause Miss Mabel continues, "I was despicable today in how I talked to the children and you. There was no reason why I was so unreasonable and suspicious about the children. Please, forgive me? I really do want to be your friend."

"Oh, Miss Mabel, we understand your situation and the discomfort your rheumatism causes. We are not offended," Gramma replies.

"Good, I'll leave now before it gets too dark. I wish you all a pleasant evening, good-bye." Miss Mabel finishes as she turns to leave.

"Auntie Mabel, please stay, I will walk you back home with a flashlight so you won't trip," Mae Lee interjects, surprising everyone.

The elderly visitor seems frozen in surprise, "You called me 'Auntie.' Why did you do that?"

Mae Lee responds with a pleading look in her eyes, "In the country where I was born, we call all adults that are friends of the family 'auntie' or 'uncle.' I hope that didn't make you unhappy. Please stay, pleeeeeease!"

"Yes, we all want you to stay for a while by the fire with us," Gramps says as he joins in the conversation at the door. "I'll walk you home, later."

"Well, I must say it looks very cozy and I think I need to be with people more in a social way. Maybe I won't be so grouchy all the time, even to myself. Thank you, I'll stay for a while." All make room, offer her the most comfortable seat in the living room, and make sure she gets some hot chocolate and a peanut butter sandwich with homemade jam.

"Before we start with our story, let's have an evening prayer and blessing on our food to welcome the Sabbath," Gramma continues. "Dear Lord of the Sabbath, the day of rest for our spiritual souls. Please bless us with Your presence and help us to think Your thoughts. Thank You, for the beauty of the sunset and that we have a friend to share this time with You. May all that we say and do bind us closer more to You. We thank You for hearing and answering this prayer. Amen."

> In the country where I was born, we call all adults that are friends of the family 'auntie' or 'uncle.' I hope that didn't make you unhappy.

"Now the story, Gramps. I've been wondering all evening about the bridge that's not there and why it is important," says Sam.

"Okay, Sam, but first a little background information. Joseph Bates was called the Apostle of the Sabbath. That was because once he learned that the Sabbath really was the seventh day of the week, like it says in the Ten Commandments, he was convinced that he should keep it sacred and share that information with everyone who would listen. Joseph first read about the true Sabbath in a little pamphlet written by T. M. Preble in 1845. He wasn't quite convinced about it, but when he heard that there were Adventist Sabbath keepers in Washington, New Hampshire, he started out walking there by himself. It is a 135 mile walk and it probably took him about forty-five hours of walking to get there. That just goes to show you the determination and toughness that Joseph had when he made up his mind to do something. He arrived at the destination, Frederick Wheeler's residence, in the evening and woke everyone up. Bates was so eager to learn about the Sabbath that Frederick got up and studied the Sabbath truth all night with him.

"The next day, the two men went to Cyrus Farnsworth's home by Millen Pond, not far from the first Sabbath-keeping Adventist church. Together the three men sat under the shade of some trees and studied more into the history of the Sabbath until Joseph was convinced that the seventh-day Sabbath was the true day to worship. On his trip home, when he crossed that important bridge that's no longer there, he met a friend, James Madison Monroe Hall. Hall asked him what the news was. Bates quickly responded, 'The news is that the seventh day is the Sabbath.' After a short time, Hall became a convert to the Sabbath doctrine, too. So someone tell me, why is that missing bridge so important?"

Dave cautiously suggested, "Maybe it's because James Hall was Joseph's first convert to the Sabbath truth."

"I think that's as good a reason as any," returns Gramps.

Auntie Mabel speaks up at this point, "I never heard that story before and I've lived not far from that bridge all my life! This will give me something to think about tonight when I go home, besides myself. I thank you for your friendship. I think I'll go now."

"I have a little brochure on the history of the Sabbath and Biblical support for it. I'll get it for you to read later and then walk you home, Mabel," Gramps adds. After they leave, Gramma, Sam, Dave, and Mae Lee pray thanking God for this new friendship with Auntie Mabel and ask that God help her to discover the full story of God's love for her.

CHAPTER FIVE

Sabbath morning dawns clear and sunny due to a steady breeze from the north. All are looking forward to the visitors who are going to arrive later in the morning. The family is up, dressed, and hungry for breakfast quite early. Then, Gramps' cell phone chimes, creating a little stir as everybody tries to find where the sound is coming from. Once found, Gramps takes it to a quiet place away from the kitchen. Everyone wonders who the caller could be. When he finally returns, Gramma asks, "Was it our visitors for the day wondering how to find the Bates' Home?"

"It was them, but that's not the issue. If you don't mind waiting a bit, I'm going to suggest we have worship first before I tell the reason for the call," answers Gramps. "Please everyone gather in the living room. Sam, would you get the New Living Translation Bible and read Acts 8:26–39. It's about an exciting adventure that one of the very first deacons in the brand-new Christian church had in evangelism travel."

"Sure," Sam replies, "I'm a traveling man myself."

> *As for Philip, an angel of the Lord said to him, "Go south down the desert road that runs from Jerusalem to Gaza." So he started out, and he met the treasurer of Ethiopia, a eunuch of great authority under the Kandake, the queen of Ethiopia. The eunuch had gone to Jerusalem to worship, and*

he was now returning. Seated in his carriage, he was reading aloud from the book of the prophet Isaiah. The Holy Spirit said to Philip, "Go over and walk along beside the carriage." Philip ran over and heard the man reading from the prophet Isaiah. Philip asked, "Do you understand what you are reading?" The man replied, "How can I, unless someone instructs me?" And he urged Philip to come up into the carriage and sit with him. The passage of Scripture he had been reading was this: "He was led like a sheep to the slaughter. And as a lamb is silent before the shearers, he did not open his mouth. He was humiliated and received no justice. Who can speak of his descendants? For his life was taken from the earth. The eunuch asked Philip, "Tell me, was the prophet talking about himself or someone else?" So beginning with this same Scripture, Philip told him the Good News about Jesus. As they rode along, they came to some water, and the eunuch said, "Look! There's some water! Why can't I be baptized?" He ordered the carriage to stop, and they went down into the water, and Philip baptized him. When they came up out of the water, the Spirit of the Lord snatched Philip away. The eunuch never saw him again but went on his way rejoicing.

"Would you like to be that kind of traveling man, Sam?" asks Gramps.

"I don't know, but I'd sure like to see a DVD of it, though," returns Sam.

Gramps says, "I don't have access to that, but I'm going to tell you another similar story about Joseph Bates. You see, Bates let the Lord lead him in ways that were much like Philip's. In the 1850s he made an evangelistic trip to Michigan. He had a dream that he was back sailing on a ship and that he should get off at Battle Creek. When he woke up, Joseph asked Dan Palmer in Jackson, Michigan, where Battle Creek was and if there were any Adventists there. Dan told him that it was forty miles away and that there weren't any Adventists there. Joseph told Palmer, 'I must go there; for in my dream I was told there was work there for me to do.' So, he got on a train going that direction and he got off at Battle Creek, which was only a small town of about two thousand people at that time.

"He didn't know anyone there, so prayed for the Lord to give him light. He heard an answer in his mind, 'Go at once and inquire of the postmaster for the most honest man in town. He will give you the name and address of the man with whom you are to work.' The postmaster suggested that David Hewitt was that man and of course being a mailman knew his address. It was early in the morning, and as Joseph knocked at this man's door, he

found him just ready for breakfast. Joseph told David, 'I have been directed to you as the most honest man in town. If this is so, I have some important truth to present to you.' Immediately, David remembered the Bible verse, 'Be not forgetful to entertain strangers for thereby some have entertained angels unaware.' So he invited Joseph in for breakfast. After the meal, he invited Joseph to have morning worship and then said, 'Now let us hear what you have to tell us.' Joseph had a preaching

chart of time prophecies that he hung up on the wall. He told David the whole story of the Second Advent Movement, then onto the Sabbath truth, and the third angel's message. Joseph recorded that, 'The most honest man in town and his wife were convinced.' They kept the next Sabbath at their home, which later became a church for believers in that area.

"Battle Creek eventually became the headquarters of the Seventh-day Adventist work for over half a century. It was here that the health, educational, and publishing work began and spread to the world. Joseph, much later, became the first president of the newly formed Michigan Seventh-day Adventist Conference. All this began with a dream, a willingness to listen, and the courage to make it happen. God has a place for each of you in His work. If you listen to His voice speaking through the Holy Spirit, you will find that place of joyful service, too."

> « If God helped Philip and Bates know what to say, I think He can help me to say the words right. »

"Wow! Another cool story about Joseph Bates, I like how God's dream for him started on a boat traveling across land. Now can you tell us the rest of the story about the phone call this morning?" asks Mae Lee.

"Well, Miss Curiosity, I'm glad you liked that story because the phone call is the reason I have to ask you a question. Are you ready for it?" asks Gramps.

"I heard that curiosity killed the cat," Mae Lee added with a little concern.

With a chuckle, Gramps responds "But satisfaction brought him back! No cat or girl will be harmed in any way. There I go again using clichés carelessly, sorry.

"The visitors called to say that there was a problem with their visit. Most of the people in the tour group cannot speak or understand much English. They have a translator with them, but she got a migraine headache this morning and can't come. Since they all speak Chinese and you speak Chinese, I was wondering if you would be willing to translate what

I say to them? I will go slow, stop after each sentence or two, and repeat it if needed. I can give you a little time to think it over, but I need to call them back soon."

Mae Lee sat quietly for a while, looking up towards the ceiling, and finally spoke, "If God helped Philip and Bates know what to say, I think He can help me to say the words right. If you pray for me, I think I can do it, but I need to stay right by you the whole time. If I make a mistake, I can hide my face behind you."

"Mae Lee, you are so brave! We will kneel now and pray. Dear Lord and Father of all peoples in the world, because you know all their languages, we know that you can help Mae Lee. Please give her the courage and a happy, smiling face. We're sure all our visitors will love her even if she forgets a word. They will be so happy that she is helping them. We pray this in Jesus' name, and for his sake, we do this. Amen."

"With Mae Lee's okay, I'm going to call our visitors back with a green light, while the rest of you help Gramma get breakfast. What do you say to that?" Gramps asks. However, no words are spoken and the kids just jump up and run to the kitchen. "Guess, that was my answer," Gramps chuckles.

CHAPTER SIX

"WELCOME TO THE Historic Joseph Bates Home," said Gramps to the new arrivals. Mae Lee, getting a nod from Gramps, bows slightly from the shoulders and repeats his words in Chinese, "你们好 *nǐmen hǎo* (hello everyone). I will be interpreting Gramps words for you." Her familiar words bring a smile from each in the group. Stopping after every phrase or sentence for Mae Lee to restate the words, Gramps continues, "These are my grandchildren, Mae Lee, Sam, and Dave, who are visiting while their parents are on a mission trip. Joseph Bates became one of the founders of the Seventh-day Adventist Church and is the reason we have this site today. We will tell more of that story later. To begin our tour, we are going to step around to the front of the house. This home was built in 1742 and consisted of two main rooms, when the Bates moved here, fifty years later in 1793. Those rooms were the room on the lower level to the right, and one just above it. So, the living space was much smaller than what you see today. They were a family of eight, soon to be nine. The home was built in the middle of a field or pasture and received the name of Meadow Farm. Can you imagine nine people spending most of their time in a two-room house? The family soon added on to make more room for the family. Today, the home has about fourteen rooms, some of them added much later than when the Bates family lived here. Inside we will show you the two rooms that have been restored to be as they would have been when the family lived here. Joseph was one year old when his family moved here. Try to imagine a family of seven brothers and sisters running around playing and working in this yard.

"There were very few trees then, and no houses between here and the river. So it would have been easy to see the tall sailing ships come and go in the harbor, now just two blocks away. They came from many different parts of the world. This river harbor was then one of the busiest in America. His father had moved the family here to improve his business opportunities as a merchant and trader. He did not sail on those ships in the harbor, but he did buy things from them to sell to others who needed them. However, the needs of home life were largely supplied by the family, themselves. Growing a garden, planting fruit trees, making clothing for the family, cutting wood for the fire, raising chickens, milking the cow, and building additions to the home were largely done by the family members. They did not run to the store every other day to pick up more supplies. Roads were unpaved, making them muddy in wet weather and dusty in dry. Trips away from home were infrequent for most family members had chores to perform. Let's move inside the house now, to continue our tour.

"This first room we call the Bustling Harbor room. We want our visitors to understand what living here would have been like in the late 1700s and early 1800s. It was not part of the first home, but added later as a separate building, known as a Summer Kitchen. Probably added after the Bates' time, it is still of interest to those learning about life in the early 1800s. The room and fireplace to the left was built separately from the main house. Can anyone guess why a separate building?"

"To keep the summer heat away from the main house in hot weather?" asks Sam.

"What about because kitchen fires sometimes got out of control and burned the building down, having a separate kitchen meant it was not as likely to destroy the whole house, right?" responds Dave.

"Right on both counts! Glad you're thinking this through," Gramps returns. "You will notice on the brick wall there were two fireplace openings, one now bricked in. Heat from this fireplace heated the oven space above it that is now covered by this steel door. This would provide space for baking bread and such. Other foods would be cooked in pots hung over the fire on this boom that can swing into the room or over the fire. This room of our museum is designed to resemble a general store or warehouse with products local families and sailors might need. In these drawers over here we have samples of many of the items Joseph might have been familiar with back then. Feel free to open the drawers and feel the contents. There were no

supermarkets, no goods wrapped in bubble-wrap or plastic bags, no refrigerators, no electric lights, no cell phones, computers, video games or prepackaged foods. Food items were either displayed in barrels or boxes or hung from the rafters, and were usually measured out by weight or quantity and hand-written records were kept. There were no American dollars or cents to use. Items for sale were often purchased with currency from other countries, or traded for other goods.

"New Bedford (this area was called New Bedford then, not Fairhaven), was one of the busiest harbors in America at the time, receiving ships from many parts of the world and trading valuable goods to the residents of a growing society. New Bedford was once known as the 'Whaling Capitol of the World.' Whale oil was much sought after as a fuel for lamps and lighting. Electricity had not yet been invented so whale oil burned brightly and cleanly not only in North America, but also in Europe and other parts of the world. Thousands of whales were slaughtered to satisfy this demand for 'clean' lighting."

Mae Lee asks, "What does the word 'slaughtered' mean?"

Gramps, knowing that Mae Lee will not like the meaning of it, says, "killed."

As predicted, Mae Lee's bottom lip starts to quiver and tears start to come, but she manages to control herself, takes a deep breath, and finishes translating the sentence. Gramps hugs her and goes on.

"As Joseph grew up here, he surely felt the excitement of visiting the wharfs and shipyards along the river, talking with sailors, and hearing the stories of adventures they had in the exotic places. He heard stories of encounters with storms, icebergs, pirates, and shipwrecks. He noted the behavior of sailors who had too much to drink. He watched shipbuilders as they put together sailing ships. He crossed the river by ferry until a bridge was finally built across the river. He helped his dad manage that bridge and collect toll (payment) from those who crossed it. There was a different cost for each of the following: a pedestrian, a horse, a cart, a wagon, a cow, a pig, chickens, etc. Joseph probably helped collect these fees. He developed a strong desire to become a sailor himself. His father, however, did not want this kind of life for his son. He knew that sailors developed nasty habits like getting drunk, cursing, swearing, chewing tobacco, living unhealthy angry lives, and wasting their money on gambling and loose living in foreign ports. When Joseph was almost fifteen, his father relented and let him take a short sailing trip to Boston Harbor with his uncle, hoping that would cure Joseph of the desire to go to sea. However, it had the opposite effect, making Joseph even more desirous of becoming a sailor. He was finally allowed to leave home and began a sailing career that would last for twenty-one years."

Sam leaned over and said in a hushed whisper, "Sounds exciting. Want to run away to sea with me?"

"Not really, I've read the rest of that story. Just listen to what Gramps says happened to Joseph," Dave responds.

After a long look over at the teens, Gramps continues, "We step now into our next room to learn more about the seagoing years of Joseph Bates. He wrote extensively about his years in his autobiography. You will see other passing ships, and as you look up through the grated hatch you will see the ship's mast and rigging rising above the ship, and clouds floating past. Please take a seat on one of the crates and you will view a short introductory video on Joseph's seagoing years. This video will be only five to eight minutes long and will briefly summarize his seagoing years. As you exit the boat room, you will enter an exhibit of the voyages Bates took and the routes will be described on the walls. On his second voyage, which was destined for Russia, his ship rammed an iceberg in the night that badly damaged the ship, and the sailors were sure they were going to die. Providentially, they survived and continued to England/Ireland for repairs. Continuing this journey, their ship was captured by Danish privateers, who were then at war with Great Britain. The captain, wanting to save his ship and cargo from the king of Denmark, commanded his crew to lie, saying they had no contact with the British. Joseph, being the youngest of the crew, was called first to testify in court. The judge showed him a box with three holes in it. The Judge stated that the box was designed to cut off the thumb and two forefingers of anyone who lied to the court. I'm sure Joseph looked at those three fingers before he put them into the holes in the box, and thought about his desire to keep them attached to his hand. Despite the captain's demand that he lie, he decided to tell the truth. Honesty was a life-long trait of Joseph. Though the captain lost his ship and his cargo, Joseph kept his fingers. The other crew members told the truth as well.

"Now Joseph was without a ship and wanted to get home. He sought a ship going to America. None were headed there directly, so he ended up catching a ride on another ship to Liverpool, England where he intended to book passage to America. While waiting for his passage, he was again captured, this time by the British, and impressed (forced to work) into the British Navy. As a result of his many escape attempts, Joseph ended up in Dartmoor Prison until the end of the 'War of 1812' which happened in 1815." Pointing to the door on display in the museum's International Travels Room, Gramps continues, "This is a door from Dartmoor Prison where Joseph was kept prisoner during America's second war with Great Britain.

"International Travel's Room illustrates the stories behind Joseph's many trips to South America, often carrying food products to starving communities. Now as captain, it was during one of these voyages, that Joseph again risked his life to protect four Brazilian passengers from Argentinian privateers. On another voyage to South America, he went to great inconvenience to return money he had received in overpayment for one of his shipments. This showed how determinedly honest he was.

"THE BOYHOOD FAMILY PARLOR is our next stop. It brings us to the first of the two original rooms restored to the historical time of the Bates' Home. A fireplace at one end would have provided both cooking facility and heat for the home in the wintertime. 'Post-and-beam' is the term used to describe this style of house-building. Upright posts were placed at the corners and horizontal beams spanned the distance between them, top and bottom. The siding was then fastened between the beams forming the outside walls. In this case, boards about one-and-a-half inches thick and twelve to twenty inches wide form the outside wall with no insulation or studs. Behind the glass on the ceiling, you can see some of the original beam and joist construction. There would have been only candles or oil lamps for lighting. The walls and ceiling were generally light-colored to allow better reflection of light. The interior walls were lath and plaster or sometimes vertical boards as we will see in another room. The fireplace also served as the cooking area where meals were prepared until a more formal kitchen was built later. This parlor would have been where much of the family life took place and visitors made welcome. Furnishings were simple and often of varied origins. The most important part of this room would be the family members who lived here. Some furnishings were imported from Europe, but most would have been constructed by local craftsmen. The boards on the floor are probably the same ones that Joseph would have walked on as he grew up.

"Next, those of you with good knees and balance will go upstairs to the parents' bedroom. It is the same size and style as this room, only with bedroom furnishings. The stairway is very steep and there is no handrail, so be careful. For those of you not making this stop you may wait for our return. In this bedroom, there are several artifacts of interest. The rope bed in the corner supplied the most comfortable accommodations for rest. Two-hundred-fifty feet of rope woven between the side and end pieces of the bed bring to mind the expression 'sleep tight, don't let the bed bugs bite.' If the ropes under the mattress were not occasionally tightened, the bed would sag, making it uncomfortable. So, this wooden tightening key was used periodically to twist and tighten the rope. Of course, the feather tick or straw mattress was susceptible to harboring bedbugs. Some ask, does everybody sleep in this one room? Traditionally all but the youngest child would sleep in the attic. There, they might hope to find a little heat from the fireplace chimney on a cold night. There was no fireplace heat as in the other rooms. The rooms were often cold because of there being no insulation, in spite of a fire, or in the absence of a fire at night. That meant your bed would be cold. Their solution was to put some hot coals from the fire in a bed-warmer (an item that looks liked a long-handled frying pan with a lid) and move it between the sheets of your bed before you climb in. The youngest child would probably occupy this room with the parents. It would also be the place where mother spun yarn or sewed clothing.

"The MILLER ROOM shows the impact that William Miller's preaching of the soon coming of Christ in the clouds of glory had on Bates. He became a Millerite preacher himself and a leader in many of their conferences.

"The October 22, 1844 date came and went without Christ's return. It has been remembered as the Great Disappointment and became a turning point in Bates' life. The focus of his Bible study now was to find out what this prophetic time period of 2,300 years was really describing.

"The SABBATH truth that God's day of rest was the seventh day of the week as described in the Ten Commandments, also became Bates' focus of Bible study.

"The LEGACY ROOM illustrates Bates' life later in the Seventh-day Adventist Church, that Joseph helped found, grew, and expanded in territory. Eventually, it moved its headquarters to Battle Creek, Michigan. Joseph Bates moved to a nearby town in Michigan where the members provided him with a small farm. He continued to travel and work for the building up of the church, helped organize the first Seventh-day Adventist Conference. He never returned to Fairhaven after moving to Michigan. In good health, he continued to preach until just a few weeks before his death, a short time before his eightieth birthday. He leaves to us a church that has been blessed by God with an expectation of Christ's soon coming, a world-wide church organization, a health message second to none, hospital and educational systems that have helped shape our world. This room outlines the legacy of this man in the years following his departure from Fairhaven. Though encouraged to retire and rest in his later years, he continued to insist on proclaiming Bible truth, as he understood it. That concludes our formal tour. You are welcome to spend more time with the exhibits and we would be happy to try to answer questions."

After finishing the last sentence, Mae Lee stands quietly, looking down at her feet. The whole group of visitors starts clapping and a few pat Mae Lee on the shoulder, smiling. "It sounds like you did a super good job of translating, Mae Lee," Gramps responds with a smile, too. Mae Lee just bows slightly and says "thank you" in Chinese. One of the ladies hands her a red envelope with bright gold Asian designed figures on it. Mae Lee bows even deeper and repeats her Chinese "thank you" several more times.

After the group leaves, Sam and Dave start questioning Mae Lee, "What's in the envelope? Is it money? If so, how did you know?"

"Yes, it will be some gift of money, because that is their custom to put gifts in this type of envelope, but I shouldn't keep it because I didn't do anything but talk," responds Mae Lee.

Gramps interjects, "Usually, any donations go directly to help support the Bates' Home. I never accept personal gifts, however, I could tell that our Chinese friends might have been very upset if I insisted that they not give it to you. Why don't you just hang on to it for a while and then later decide what to do with it. I'm sure that would make our visitors happy."

"Time for lunch before we get anymore visitors," calls Gramma. Not needing another invitation, all start off to the house in a quick trot.

CHAPTER SEVEN

"Gramma, it was so exciting!" says Mae Lee.

"And lucrative for Mae Lee," adds Dave.

"The epitome of elucidative expression," announces Sam. Everyone pauses and stares at Sam with a look between amusement and admiration.

"Where did you find those words? On the back of a cereal box or something?" asks Gramma.

"No one really understands my need to express myself in my true native vocabulary," replies Sam with a look of hurt pride. After a period of silence with all staring at Sam, he says, "Okay, I read it somewhere and it sounded too cool to forget. Just wait, someday, I'll be able to speak that language, all the time."

"Tell me when you plan to start doing that, so I can carry a dictionary around with me while in your presence, Sir Elocution. Right now it appears that you are inebriated with the exuberance of your own verbosity," continues Gramps.

"Please stop. We need to eat and talk about what we will be doing after we close the museum later this afternoon," enjoins Gramma. After the blessing on the food, and much of the meal eaten in delicious silence, Gramma ventures a suggestion for later, "We need to take the kids to Phoenix Park. It isn't far away, has a lot of history, is along a beautiful beach, and has hungry seagulls everywhere!"

Mae Lee stops eating and starts bouncing up and down, chanting, "Let's go now! Let's go now!"

Gramps replies, "Soon, fair lady, but we have to wait and see if we get any more visitors. Also, with all the excitement we've been having lately, I think we all need to rest for a little while." After several votes to affirm the plan, all settle down to finish the afternoon meal. Then each seeks out a quiet place to read and rest.

After the sun leaves its zenith and descends to an appropriate arch, Gramma loudly announces, "Time to gather what we want and take off for our destination."

In less than ten seconds, Mae Lee is standing beside her, wearing a backpack with Bagel riding on top, and questions, "Can I get the crackers and bread for the seagulls, now?"

"Yes, do that. Sam, remember your camera, and Dave, would you wake up Gramps?" directs Gramma. When all are in the car, they drive the few miles to the park. The beauty of the park and the possibilities that it offers, especially with the large flocks of sea birds gathered there, result in silent adoration. The family is not alone; there are several others strolling along the beach, looking at the stone wall and canons facing out towards the bay, or seated on park benches along the edge.

> *All of a sudden, Mae Lee notices something that she's never seen before: a woman walking a black, fluffy cat on a leash heading toward a bench nearby to her.*

All of a sudden, Mae Lee notices something that she's never seen before: a woman walking a black, fluffy cat on a leash heading toward a bench nearby to her. Since curiosity doesn't just live inside cats, Mae Lee, overcome with it, gravitates towards this unusual sight, and asks a question, "How did you teach your cat to walk on a leash?"

The pleasant, slightly greying haired lady dressed in denim slacks and shirt stops and seems to notice Mae Lee for the first time. "Well, well,

so we have a kitty cat lover here. What's up kid?" the smiling questioner asks in what one might call a "Boston accent." "Your shiny black hair pretty much matches Lucy's. You want to pet her? Let me grab a bench heah [here] first, I need to take a weight off my dogs [feet]. Don't you just love this pahk [park]?" Approaching cautiously and bending down to the level of the interesting kitty, Mae Lee slowly extends one hand for the green-eyed beauty to smell. "So, you know how to make friends with felines; you're a cat person like me! I'm into 'em [them] big time." Pausing, the lady looks around searchingly. "So where's ya Mum [your mother]?"

Mae Lee chuckling responds, "You don't see anyone who looks like me, right?"

Gramma, seeing the concerned look in the lady's face, approaches them to help solve the issue, "Mae Lee belongs to us, we're her grandparents, and those two teen-agers are her brothers."

Smiling with comprehension on how this family could fit together, the lady continues, "I'm Patsy, a volunteer at the Fairhaven Animal Shelter, and I live in an old Victorian-style home with a widow's walk, a couple blocks from here. Where ya [do you] come from?"

"My husband and I are docents at the Captain Joseph Bates Museum, and our grandchildren are visiting us while their parents are on a short mission trip," Gramma replies.

"My Mum [mother] use ta [used to] tell me about that place before it was a museum, oldest house in town, she said, I've wanted to see it fuh days [for a long time]," Patsy adds.

"Can you come this week, before we leave?" Mae Lee quickly asks.

"Great idear [idea], would love ta [to do that] kid," Patsy replies.

Mae Lee, full of wonderment about the beautiful cat, asks, "Is this your pet?"

"Wish I could keep all the felines that come into the shelter, but I gotta grump [have a grouchy person] for a landlord, he says no way, Jose! I'm just training this one to help get it a home. People roun heah [around here] don't have much lawn, and there's too many caas [cars]. Yeh hafta sashay em [You have to walk them] on leashes to let them smell the water at the pahk [park]. Beautiful place, this Phoenix Pahk [park]. Myself, I come here everyday. If'n you can hunkah down heah [If you can sit here] awhile kid, I'll tell you about it," Patsy offers.

With a look to Gramma for permission and receiving a nod, Mae Lee replies, "Let me first go get my Gramps and brothers. I'm sure they'll want to hear this."

In a short time, the family is seated on the bench with Patsy or on the ground close enough to hear the story while the fragrance of the sea and the call of the seagulls surround them, creating the appropriate ambiance.

After all are introduced, Patsy begins, "Ova thah [over there], are the cannons with a story all their own. You see, it was on May 13–14, 1775, that the first naval battle of the American Revolution took place off this shore! It was when Nathaniel Pope and Daniel Egery captured two British sloops on Buzzard's Bay. Aftah [after] that, the town constructed a fort to protect the haabah [harbor]. It had eleven cannons that had been captured in the Bahamas by John Paul Jones. You see, the Brits were smaaht [smart], they snuck in 4,000 troops into New Bedford on September 5–6, 1778, and came south through Fairhaven. Then they attacked, and what with only thirty-four locals to defend it, the fort was taken and burned. They smashed all the cannons, except one. Latah [later], the fort was rebuilt and named Fort Phoenix because it arose from ashes. In June of 1814, near the end of the Waah [War] of 1812, the American troops repelled the British when they attacked. During the Civil Waah [War], eight twenty-four-pound cannons were put heah [here], five of which remain at the fort, today. In 1926, it was purchased for the town by Lady Fairhaven, Mrs. Urban H. Broughton of England, a daughta' [daughter] of the town's benefacta'[benefactor] Henry Huttleston Rogers. Since then, it's been preserved by the town as a public pahk [park]. In 1973, it was placed on the National Register of Historic Places. So there you have it! History sittin right unda' ya [sitting right under you]. Suga [Mae Lee], did I heah [hear] right, you got food for those seagulls?"

With a squeal of "Yes!" Mae Lee jumps up, grabs her backpack with Bagel clinging precariously on top, and runs off to find a good feeding site. Looking at the family still seated, Patsy quips, "She's quite the caad [card], isn't she?"

A pleasant Sabbath evening was spent with Patsy as all took part in feeding the gulls, enjoying the breezes of the bay, and reading the historical markers and signs. When the sun's setting rays began to throw splashes of crimson and gold through the horizon, many of the sea admirers had left, leaving quietness behind, Gramps suggests going back over by the bench where they first had gathered. When seated, Gramps asks Patsy, "Would you like to join us for a sunset worship time, right here?

I have a story to tell about Captain Joseph Bates, that you might find interesting."

"Sure, Captain, go ahead. I enjoy the pahk [park] best at sunset, anyways," she replies. Little Lucy, having gotten tired, curls up on Patsy's lap and quietly goes to sleep while purring.

After a pause of silent prayer, Gramps begins, "In the early 1840s, in upstate New York near the border with Vermont, another captain, this time a military captain, William Miller, made an outstanding discovery while reading the Bible. His finding led to the understanding that Jesus was going to be coming soon. This was unlike what most churches believed because they thought Jesus could only come after 1,000 years of peace. This understanding of Jesus' soon return spread throughout America, ending up with about one million people expecting Jesus to come on October 22, 1844, because of the prophecies found in Daniel and Revelation. One of those people was Captain Joseph Bates, by then a retired sea captain. Bates arranged for William Miller to preach right here in Fairhaven on March 15–18, 1841. Later, Bates traveled many miles to preach that same message and then, along with many others, was greatly disappointed when Jesus didn't appear as expected.

"This disappointment was followed by years of Bible research to find out where they had gone wrong. What they found out was that they were right about the time, but wrong about the event. God had put those prophecies in the Bible to let people know that the end time judgment was to begin on that date in 1844. Also, through intense Bible study, people found out that the seventh-day Sabbath, as mentioned in the Ten Commandments, was the day that God had arranged for people to meet with Him in worship. This was a revolutionary thought because most people worshiped on Sunday, a day that had been set up to combine pagan worship and Christian worship by the Roman Emperor, Constantine. God had never changed His law—it was to last forever because it is a transcript of His character."

Mae Lee interrupts with a question, "What do you mean by a *transcript*?"

"Good question, Mae Lee," Gramps continues. "It tells what God values and how He wants us to live and worship together.

"In the early 1850s after William Miller had passed away, Joseph Bates made a trip to the home of Captain William Miller. He was graciously received by Miller's widow, Lucy, and she asked him to speak in the small, white, wooden clapboard chapel that William Miller had built on his farm in 1848. At that Sunday evening service, Bates explained about the Sabbath being really Saturday, not Sunday. He did such a clear presentation, that Lucy said that she couldn't help but admit that it was right. Later, it was disclosed that William Miller's son, Solomon, and his wife, Wealthy, became Sabbath keepers, probably from hearing Bates' explanation of the Sabbath. Bates was the first of the Advent believers to keep the seventh day Sabbath and traveled widely to preach it at his own expense. Bates still expected Jesus to come soon and wanted people to understand what God was like so that the Holy Spirit could help them grow to be more like Jesus everyday and be ready for His coming.

"Let's all bow our heads in prayer, please. Dear Lord and Savior of all, we come to You in faith, believing that You have a mission for each of us as You did for Joseph Bates. We thank You for the gift of the Sabbath, this hallowed time filled with Your presence in a special way more than any other day of the week. Please help us to grow into Your likeness and find some way to spread the good news of Your love and soon return to someone this week. For in Jesus' name we ask this, please. Amen."

"That was just wonderful, just wonderful, wouldn't have missed it for the world!" Patsy celebrates.

"Patsy, how would you like to come over this evening and get your own private tour of the Joseph Bates Home and have a light supper with us?" questions Gramma.

"Yes, please come, I would like you to bring Lucy, too," adds Mae Lee pleadingly. "I'd like to play with her."

"I could bring something along, what would you like: grindahs, frappes, tonic, pup-con, or ice cream with jimmies on top?" This request was answered with a silence as each tries to digest the words' meanings.

Finally, Gramma answers, "Just bring yourself, we've got plenty to eat."

"OK, I'll be there after I go home and get some food for Lucy. I wouldn't miss this for a 'baax a quaataas.' See you in a shake," replies their guest.

Patsy was off at a trot, when Gramps calls out, "Do you want directions on how to get to the museum?"

"I'll be ova thah, probably before you … know every inch of Fairhaven, lived near heah most all my life, I knows most everyone in it, too. Be there in a jiff." Patsy puffs as she strides quickly away.

"Guess we better get moving to get there before our guest does," chuckles Gramps.

Arriving home, the family thinks about what to serve for supper. "Wish you had let Patsy bring the food. I don't know for sure what she said, but it sounded good," says Sam.

"I think 'pup-con' was popcorn and not sure of the rest," adds Dave.

"I have an 'idear'! What about tomato, cheese, lettuce sandwiches?" asks Mae Lee.

"You sure pick up new vocabulary words quickly," comments Gramma. "Sam and Dave would you please make a fresh fruit smoothie to go with the sandwiches? And Gramps, what about another fire in the fireplace? There's a cool breeze coming in off the Bay." Soon all are busy, when a knock interrupts the preparations. Gramma and Mae Lee answer the door to find a reoccurring surprise. Auntie Mabel stands there with a box. "Good to see you again, come in, Mabel," Gramma invites. "We're just getting a little meal together, be glad to share it with you."

"I didn't mean to be a party crasher—just wanted to give you a little something I made," responds their neighbor as she gives the box to Mae Lee. A wonderful chocolate chip cookie fragrance fills the room when the box is opened. Mabel is almost overwhelmed with a flood of affectionate words and before she realizes it, she finds herself sitting at their table with food appearing from everywhere. Another knock brings their expected guest with the leashed pet.

Mae Lee announces, "My life is now complete! Nothing can improve it."

"That is a welcome and half! Glad to make you so happy," responds Patsy.

"Well, well, if it isn't the Polar Bear from the Bay?! Haven't seen you in a coon's age!" greets Mabel.

"Likewise, I'm sure, haven't see you fuh days [for a long time], how have ya been keepin' yourself?" responds Patsy.

"Fair to middlin', thanks to my good neighbors, here," returns Mabel.

Mae Lee comes close to Auntie Mabel and asks, "Why did you call her a Polar Bear?"

Stifling a laugh, Mabel answers, "Because, when a person has the gumption and stamina to jump in the Bay wearing nothing but a swimsuit in the month of January, we call them Polar Bears instead of insane."

"Now Mabel, don't go puttin' down our Polar Bear Club until you try it for yourself," Patsy coolly remonstrates.

Gramma lightens the mood by announcing, "Supper is served!" After the blessing, all heartily join in the feast.

"Best suppah ever!" announces Patsy, "sandwich and frappe."

《 *Mabel is the first to speak, "A child and a kitten were made for each other."* 》

"Now I know what to order if I want a milkshake in Fairhaven," Dave quietly whispers to Sam.

While the discussion continues, Mae Lee, pulling a piece of yarn across the rug that's being chased by a fluffy, green-eyed huntress, is so enchanted with playing with the cat that she misses the conversation. However, the diners do not miss the joy in Mae Lee's eyes. Mabel is the first to speak, "A child and a kitten were made for each other," and then asks, "Patsy, could she keep the kitten here for a few days until they leave?"

"I don't see why not; it would be good for them both. I'm too busy most of the time to be much company for the Kitty," answers Patsy.

Mae Lee does not miss THIS conversation, with an eager questioning look to Gramma, she waits for the answer with bated breath. "Well, will you do all the care and feeding necessary for it, night and day?" responds Gramma.

"Yes, yes, yes! I'd be even more happy than I already am, even though I don't know how that is possible," promises Mae Lee.

The cozy evening quietly winds down, Gramma takes Patsy for a short tour of the museum, and all begin to think about calling it a day. Patsy prepares to leave and promises to return soon with little Lucy's dishes, food, and kitty litter pan before retiring for the night. With that accomplished and all are home in bed for the evening, Mae Lee lies awake; thinking for a long while with Lucy snuggled up close. Pictures of the happenings of the day float quickly by over and over: the Chinese group, the money in an envelope, the park with feeding seagulls, worship by the seashore, a yummy supper, and most of all a chubby warm kitten snuggled up close. "Thank you, Jesus. Watch over all the other orphans back in my country, please find them homes as good as this. I love you so much, and they need to know You love them, too. Amen."

CHAPTER EIGHT

Sea Fever (published in 1902)

"I must go down to the seas again, to the lonely sea and the sky,
And all I ask is a tall ship and a star to steer her by;
And the wheel's kick and the wind's song and the white sail's shaking,
And a grey mist on the sea's face, and a grey dawn breaking.
I must go down to the seas again, for the call of the running tide
Is a wild call and a clear call that may not be denied;
And all I ask is a windy day with the white clouds flying,
And the flung spray and the blown spume, and the sea-gulls crying.
I must go down to the seas again, to the vagrant gypsy life,
To the gull's way and the whale's way where the wind's like a whetted knife;
And all I ask is a merry yarn from a laughing fellow-rover,
And quiet sleep and a sweet dream when the long trick's over."
—by John Masefield

GRAMPS IS UP earlier than the rest this morning, reading his Bible and books about sailing. Coming across this poem, he contemplates how he could tell his grandchildren about Joseph Bates without giving a clear word picture of Bates' attraction for sailing and how important it was to this patriarch of the Adventist Church and to most people in this fledgling of the American democracy in the early 1800s. Soon he hears the distant

rumble of excited chatter and the thudding of several pairs of feet on the stairs.

"Today's the day! We sail the Bay! Whoop, whoop, hurray! Up, up, away!" Sam's exuberant, newly-created song echoes through the early morning air.

"Sam, did you forgot that it is tomorrow that we sail? Today, we go to the Whaling Museum," Gramps corrects.

"I know, but the song came to me today. I'm practicing for tomorrow!" Sam responds.

"Okay, I'll look forward to hearing it, tomorrow! Now for today, since we have the day off with our volunteer docent watching the Bates' Home, we're planning on first going to the New Bedford Whaling Museum and then I thought we'd take a drive down to Mystic

Harbor in Connecticut and see the oldest whaling ship, the *Charles W. Morgan*. It's quite a drive, but we'll take a scenic route along the bays, ending up near Block Island Sound. You see, this site has over nineteen acres with a recreated 19th century coastal village. It has things like a working shipyard and exhibit halls. The *Charles W. Morgan* is the last remaining ship of the American whaling fleet. At one time there were almost 3,000 whaling ships. This one was built in 1841 and was launched from New Bedford. She is a huge vessel. Thirty-five or so sailors would process the whale blubber. It tells an important part of our nation's history. Mystic Seaport Museum is the nation's leading maritime museum and is less than a two-hour drive if you stay near the coast. I've always wanted to go there—now I have a good excuse with this being an educational trip for my grandchildren. How's that strike you?" questions Gramps.

"You sure know a lot about this ship already; it sounds exciting. We can take books along to read, right?" requests Dave.

"In case you get bored, is that what you mean?" Gramps ends with a sigh.

"I need to have someone take care of Lucy. Oh, dear! I don't want her to be lonely without me," stresses Mae Lee.

By now, Gramma arrives and suggests, "What about asking Auntie Mabel to take care of her for the day? I think she took a shine to the kitten."

"How can she shine a cat? Lucy's fur is already shiny and sparkles in the sunlight," Mae Lee observes.

Sam answers, "Gramma means that Auntie Mabel likes Lucy, maybe more than she likes people. Okay, I shouldn't have said that last statement. I do think she's getting used to us."

"I know she likes me," Mae Lee adds, "because she talked Patsy into letting me keep Lucy for a while."

Gramma suggests, "I'll call her in a little while—it's still early. We need to be getting breakfast going, first. Last one in the kitchen is a scrambled tofu."

With breakfast over, Gramps gathers everyone in the parlor for worship. "Our text today is: Psalm 107:23–32, from The Message (MSG) Bible:

> *Some of you set sail in big ships;*
> *you put to sea to do business in faraway ports.*
> *Out at sea you saw God in action,*
> *saw his breathtaking ways with the ocean:*
> *With a word he called up the wind—*
> *an ocean storm, towering waves!*
> *You shot high in the sky, then the bottom dropped out;*
> *your hearts were stuck in your throats.*
> *You were spun like a top, you reeled like a drunk,*
> *you didn't know which end was up.*
> *Then you called out to God in your desperate condition;*
> *he got you out in the nick of time.*
> *He quieted the wind down to a whisper,*
> *put a muzzle on all the big waves.*
> *And you were so glad when the storm died down,*
> *and he led you safely back to harbor.*
> *So thank God for his marvelous love,*
> *for his miracle mercy to the children he loves.*
> *Lift high your praises when the people assemble,*
> *shout Hallelujah when the elders meet!*

"Is that exciting or what? Can you think of Bible stories where people were in ships?" asks Gramps.

Mae Lee suggests, "There was Moses in the Ark and Noah in a basket."

After a long pause, Gramma responds, "I think you got the two people switched."

Mae Lee puzzles, "I know that I heard Moses had an ark made for the sanctuary."

"Yes, but that wasn't a boat, Mae Lee," Gramma continues. "Noah's ark was a flat-bottomed ship, remember?"

"Oh, yes, sometimes I get names confused," Mae Lee returns.

"There was Jonah and the big fish, Paul in a shipwreck, Peter fishing on Galilee," Dave suggests.

"How about Jesus walking on the water to the sinking ship full of doubting disciples?" adds Sam.

Gramps continues, "In each of these God was aware of where people were—they weren't lost from His vision, and He rescued them in various ways. Let's sing the first verse and chorus to, 'Master the Tempest is Raging.'" With Gramma at the piano, the songs fill the air:

> *Master, the tempest is raging!*
> *The billows are tossing high!*
> *The sky is o'ershadowed with blackness,*
> *No shelter or help is nigh;*
> *Carest Thou not that we perish?*
> *How canst Thou lie asleep,*
> *When each moment so madly is threatening*
> *A grave in the angry deep?*
> *The winds and the waves shall obey Thy will,*
> *Peace, be still!*
> *Whether the wrath of the storm tossed sea,*
> *Or demons or men, or whatever it be*
> *No waters can swallow the ship where lies*
> *The Master of ocean, and earth, and skies;*
> *They all shall sweetly obey Thy will,*
> *Peace, be still! Peace, be still!*
> *They all shall sweetly obey Thy will,*
> *Peace, peace, be still!*

Gramps ends with prayer, "Dear Lord of land and sea, even though You hold the worlds in place and tell the waters on earth where to stop, and where to gush out of rocks, You still care about and plan our days. You astound us with Your greatness and power. You are truly an awesome God and Friend. Please watch over us and help us to learn something of value, today. We thank You for answering our prayer, because we pray in Jesus' name. Amen."

"Now, let's take along a lunch and water bottles, see if Aunt Mabel will kitty-sit Lucy, slather on suntan lotion, remember our tickets, get our GPS set, get the books we gave you ..."

Mae Lee interrupts, "Don't forget Bagel!"

"Yes, the seagull from the bay, goes, too. Meet you at the car in twenty minutes! Heave Ho! Let's go!" finishes Gramps.

When all has been arranged and stowed away, their car pulls out to make the short trip to the New Bedford Whaling Museum, since it's only one town away to the west. Gramma reads the museum's brochure: "'You'll marvel at massive whale skeletons, America's longest painting, and the world's largest collection of historical scrimshaw. Climb aboard a half scale model of a 19th century whaling vessel—the Lagoda—the world's largest ship model! Enjoy an exceptional view of the working waterfront from Harbor View Gallery on the upper level. Enjoy hands-on learning for all ages throughout the Museum and in the 3,000 sq. ft Casa dos Botes Discovery Center, where you can row an Azorean whaleboat, set sail, spot a whale from the top mast, and learn about navigation. The Discovery Center honors the legacy and heritage of the Portuguese Community.' ("Casa dos Botes" is Portuguese for "boat house.") Having been there before, I think it will take us two hours to see and experience it all. After that we'll get on the road again and discuss it along the way."

"And read our books, right?" asks Dave.

"Yes, Dave, I'd like you to read a certain section in your book as we travel. It will help pass the time quickly," adds Gramps.

Arriving at the museum was relatively quick and painless. After entering all are impressed with the massive skeletal remains of large sea creatures that are hung from the ceiling, awed by the expressive art masterpieces, educated by the signage information, and entertained by the ability to raise and lower the sails on a mock ship's deck. When most of their energy has been expanded, Gramma remembers one thing they have to see. "We must go to the place where they have a collection of old ship's logs."

Mae Lee says, "I think logs aren't that interesting, all of them look brown and round, hey, that almost rhymes, right?"

Gramma returns, "Logs refer to a ship's diary where captains would record information like the events of their voyages, cargo sold and purchased, and sometimes storms, and so on. Here they have a log written in Joseph Bates' own handwriting. Isn't that exciting!" After all get to view this prized possession, they decide to be on their way to the next stop for the day, Mystic Harbor!

Once the family pulls out of the congested traffic areas onto the larger highway, Gramps remembers Dave's book reading assignment. "Dave, would you turn to the story in Joseph's autobiography where he tells about returning to America after spending years in Dartmouth Prison in England. It's the part where they are nearing an ice field that could have sunk them. Can you find that part?"

"Sure, I've read past that already. Yes, here it is:

> As we approached the eastern edge of the banks of Newfoundland, about two-thirds of the distance across the Atlantic Ocean, I found we were in the place where I was shipwrecked by the ice several years before, as related in a previous chapter. As this perilous place became the topic of conversation, we learned that a number among us had experienced like difficulties in passing over these banks in the spring season of the year. Captain Carr said he had made fifteen voyages to Newfoundland and never had seen any ice, and he did not believe there was any in our way. In the afternoon, we saw a large patch of sheet-ice. We asked the captain what he called that. He acknowledged that it was ice. As the night set in, the wind increased to a gale from the east. Captain Carr, unmindful of all that had

been said to him respecting the danger of ice in our track, still kept the ship scudding before the gale under a close-reefed main-top-sail and foresails, determined to have his own way rather than lay by until morning, as suggested by some of the prisoners. Some thirty of us, unwilling to trust to the captain's judgment, took our position on the bow and bowsprit of the ship to look out for ice. At midnight the ship was driving furiously before the gale and storm, evidently without any hope of our having time to avoid ice if we should see it, and in danger of being dashed in pieces without a moment's warning. We also felt a marked change in the air. In this dilemma, we decided to take the ship from the captain and heave her to. We found him at the quarter-deck conning the ship. We briefly stated our dangerous position, and told him that about three hundred souls were at the mercy of his will; and now, if he did not round his ship to, we would do it for him. Seeing our determination to act in this matter immediately, he cried out to his crew, "Round in the larboard main brace! Put the helm a-starboard!" This laid the main-top-sail to the mast, and let the ship come by the wind.

This being done, the onward progress of the ship was stayed until the dawn of the morning, which showed us how narrowly we had escaped with our lives. Large islands of ice lay right in our track, and if we had continued to run before the gale we should have been in the midst of them, in imminent danger of being dashed in pieces. The willfulness of Captain Carr was now evident to all, and the course we pursued in requiring him to heave the ship to was also justifiable. And after the ship was again turned on her onward course, and passing these huge islands of ice, we were all stirred to watch until we had passed the banks and were again safe in the fathomless ocean. These bodies of ice had the appearance of large cities in the distance, and had it not been for our forethought, would in all probability have been the cause of our immediate destruction.

Moreover, a large majority of us were satisfied that this was the best time to take the ship from the captain and proceed to New York or Boston, from whence we could more readily reach our homes; for we had decided and declared, as before stated to Captain Carr, that his ship should never take us to City Point, Va., where his charter party required him to land us. Having passed beyond all danger from ice, the most difficult point for us to decide was, which of the two ports we should steer for, if we took the ship. When suddenly one of our number took the wheel from the helmsman. Captain Carr demanded that he should leave it immediately, and ordered his man to take the helm again. A number of us also urged our friend to take the helm, assuring him that we would protect him. At this Captain Carr became very much enraged, saying what he would do with us if he had a crew able to cope with us. But he saw that resistance was vain; we had taken possession of the helm, the ship therefore would no longer be steered by his direction. Seeing what was done, he called us a "rabble," "roughally," etc., for taking his ship from him on the high seas, and wished to know what we were going to do with her, and who was to be the captain. Captain Conner, of Philadelphia, was lifted up by those who stood near him, and placed with his feet on the head of the capstan (a cylinder four feet high, with levers to weigh the anchors, etc.). "There is our captain!" cried the multitude. (Bates, Joseph. *My Life and Adventures: Captain Joseph Bates*).

"So Dave, what did you learn in that section? questions Gramps.

"One thing was clear, but I didn't quite understand all the sailor's language or the names for the parts of the ship. What I found exciting was how they actually mutinied and took over the control of the ship because they had a very unwise captain who was just out to make money and was putting Joseph and the other returning P.O.W.'s (prisoners of war) at risk," Dave explains.

"Do you think that was the right thing to do?" Gramps further questions.

"Yes, because even though it was against the international law of shipping, if they hadn't done it, they may never have returned home alive. They didn't harm this criminal captain or his crew, so they were not vicious, just determined to make it home from being unjustly held as prisoners," replies Dave.

"What does that say to you, Dave?" continues Gramps.

"Sometimes, in life you have to choose between two sides when either side could result in trouble. Also, if people mistreat us, we should still be respectful and not harm them."

《 Sometimes, in life you have to choose between two sides when either side could result in trouble. 》

"Well said, Dave—try to always remember that." The rest of the trip to Mystic Harbor continued with short rest stops along the way and beautiful scenery flowing by.

Rolling up to this museum village, all are astounded by its size and multitude of possibilities for exploration. They eventually find out that it is located on the banks of Connecticut's historic Mystic River. It was founded in 1929, as a home to four vessels with National Historic Landmark status. It is an interactive experience, where one can learn about 19th-century New England's seafaring heritage and maritime history through on-site historians, storytellers, and craftspeople. They climb aboard historic vessels—including the wooden whale ship, *Charles W. Morgan*, witness shipbuilding in action in the working shipyard, duck inside the cooperage, and explore the stars (and the art of celestial navigation) at the Treworgy

Planetarium. There really isn't enough time to see it all in one day, but they really have a wonderful learning experience about shipping in the 1800s.

Closing time comes and the family is reluctantly walking back toward their car, when Sam starts staring at one of the park workers standing nearby. He stops with his mouth wide open, but with no words coming out. After sprinting over to the greying, slender, dark-skinned man, Sam stands smack dab in front of him and starts laughing and crying at the same time. The man seems transfixed in shock himself, and, finally able to get words together, asks, "Is it really you, Sammy? I never thought I'd ever find you again! Thank you, Lord Jesus." Then both hug, crying with tears of joy.

Sam, remembering his family, calls, "Come here! I've found my friend that kept me safe on the streets and taught me how to create knots. I can't believe it, but it's true." Turning to Jason, Sam gets a serious look on his face and asks, "Why did you leave me and not say good-bye?"

Jason looks down with a sad face, hesitating to answer, but finally says, "Let's sit down; it's a long story." When all are seated on a couple of adjacent benches, Sam more formally introduces his family to Jason, and explains to him why and how they are his family. Jason responds, "Praise the Lord! I've been praying for you all these years that you'd get a good family that would love and take care of you in a proper way. Do you love Jesus, Sammy?" After Sam responds with a nod yes, Jason looking up, with more tears coursing down his brown weathered cheeks continues, "Thank you, Lord, my prayers are answered! I can die now that I've seen his salvation!"

Sam, taken back by Jason's response, is silent for a while, but then comes back again with the question, "Why didn't you tell me that you were leaving?"

Looking down at his feet, Jason replies softly, "It may have looked that way, but I was there in the shadows when the Social Service workers came and took you away to find you a foster home. I told them to come that day and knew that you wouldn't have wanted that to happen. I loved you too much to keep you sleeping on the streets with me. You needed a real home with a real mom and dad who would love you and give you a future!"

With a catch in his throat Gramps asks, "I see you have a uniform on; do you work here full time?"

"Yes, I'm a retired assistant guide, but not full time, and live nearby in a senior citizen apartment," Jason answers.

Gramps continues, "Do you know anything about sailing?"

"Sure do—did it for years before I lived on the streets and traveled here and there to get my bearings on life. I found Jesus and that made all the difference," he replies.

"Well, that being the case, how about going with us for a couple of days to where we live because the kids are going to be doing their last sailing trip, on Thursday? That would give you a few days to get reacquainted before they leave," Gramps suggests.

"Thanks so much for the invitation, would love that, but I'm committed to being here for Tuesday and Wednesday. I could take a bus over to the Fairhaven harbor and be there Thursday morning. I have that day through the weekend off," Jason replies with broad grin.

"Wonderful, bring along some changes of clothing and stay with us for a few days. There is a small apartment upstairs near the Joseph Bates' Home—you could stay there," adds Gramma, "And since it's supper time now, let's all find a place to eat together. Now that you and Sam have just found each other, we need to celebrate."

"Thank you, Ma'am, I'd be most grateful for that," Jason answers with a few more tears rolling down his cheeks.

With the meal over, Jason is driven to his apartment, and after goodbye hugs, the family again climbs in their car and starts home as the sun began to set. Many of the car occupants sleep along the way. Arriving back at the home, Gramps carries the sleeping little Miss Mae Lee to her room while the others sleepily find their own separate ways to bed. In wishing them a good night, Gramps quotes again, "Have a 'quiet sleep and a sweet dream.'"

CHAPTER NINE

IF IT WASN'T for the swaying harbor buoys chiming out a wakeup call and the sunlight making patchwork designs on the sleepers' faces, the tired residents in the Joseph Bates' caretaker's home at the Bates' Museum may have slept until noon. There also was the lure of the promised sailing trip on Buzzard Bay that pulled them into a sitting position. After stumbling into appropriate sailing clothes and footwear, all made their way to the kitchen to see what nourishment could be had for this especially awaited day. Warm oatmeal with raisins and brown sugar, whole grain toast with peanut butter and banana, along with fresh sliced oranges most effectively filled the empty spot created by a long night's sleep.

"Gramma, I really need to see more seagulls and other water birds for my report. Can we plan another island picnic for our boat trip?" Mae Lee requests.

"I think that is an excellent idea! Let me see, what kind of sandwiches would be in order? What about sauerkraut sandwiches?" Gramma suggests with a twinkle in her eyes, which Mae Lee didn't see because she was sadly staring down at her remaining breakfast.

Responding after a long pause, the dejected girl says, "I don't know if I should eat something that I don't understand. What is *sauerkraut*, anyways?"

Laughing, Gramma returns, "Maybe it's German for tomato, cheese, lettuce, and mayonnaise!"

Looking up and seeing everyone's amusement, Mae Lee says, "I'm not sure I like food jokes so early in the morning!"

"I'm sorry, honey, didn't mean to upset you; I get silly sometimes when I'm tired." Gramma apologizes.

"Now I'm disappointed, no sauerkraut sandwiches! How am I ever going to be captain of my German ship?" Gramps laments.

Mae Lee jumps on his lap and starts tickling him, "You don't have to be silly, too. I make you laugh for that."

Unsuccessfully fending her off, Gramps giggles, "Stop, stop! I surrender! I promise no more non-jokes today! If everyone is done, let's clean up and have worship. Sam, would you look up Psalm 8 in The Living Bible (TLB) and meet us in the living room?"

Sam reads:

> *O Lord our God, the majesty and glory of your name fills all the earth and overflows the heavens. You have taught the little children to praise you perfectly. May their example shame and silence your enemies! When I look up into the night skies and see the work of your fingers—the moon and the stars you have made—I cannot understand how you can bother with mere puny man, to pay any attention to him! And yet you have made him only a little lower than the angels and placed a crown of glory and honor upon his head. You have put him in charge of everything you made; everything is put under his authority: all sheep and oxen, and wild animals too, the birds and fish, and all the life in the sea. O Jehovah, our Lord, the majesty and glory of your name fills the earth.*

When Sam finishes, Gramps asks, "What meaning does this have for us, today?"

Dave answers, "I think it means that people have not been doing their God assigned task! The last time we went sailing, I saw a lot of pollution and garbage in the water! I've read that many sea creatures are dying from ingesting plastics from our trash that ends up in the ocean waters. If people don't start doing something different, there will be massive die-offs of some of the most fragile of God's ocean creatures."

Gramma adds, "It has already happened in Buzzards Bay! I remember that in 2003, a Bouchard Transportation Co. barge ruptured a cargo tank and around 15,000 gallons of fuel spilled into Buzzards Bay. The oil released affected more than fifty-three miles of shoreline, primarily along the western side of Buzzards Bay. It killed

thousands of shore birds and other water creatures. To people's credit, there was a big response to help clean up the spill. Although a number of birds died as a direct result of the spill, the recovery and rehabilitation unit in New Bedford alone saved thirteen birds and released nine, but it was an awful loss!"

All sit in silent sadness for a while and then Sam asks, "That's bad, but what can we do to help prevent more of this type of pollution?"

Dave continues, "I think we need to stop plastics from getting into our water systems. We could re-use our own cloth shopping bags, avoid using plastic straws, cut down on using plastic wraps for foods, and push government agencies into making laws to prevent so much plastic waste in our environment. We shouldn't just throw up our hands and keep on doing the same environmentally destructive habits of convenience. Then we would be fulfilling our God given responsibilities as best we can!"

"Dave, go for it! Us older members of God's family have developed irresponsible self-centered habits. We need young people to wake us up to our Christian duties in caring for the earth. In scripture, God warned in Revelation 11:18 that He would destroy "those who destroy the earth." We all need to take this seriously. Thank you for your enthusiasm! Mae Lee, would you be willing to have prayer?" Gramps finishes.

"Dear God of land, sea, and sky and all the animals, fish, and birds. Help us to be Your hands and feet to take care of them all. Thank You for listening to a little girl like me. Please watch over us and keep us safe, today. Amen."

"This has been a good start to what looks like a beautiful day for sailing. What about everyone working together to get all the necessary items for our day at sea in a half hour? You might want to bring along notebooks, pens, cameras, cell phones, suntan lotions, hats, and plenty of water and delicious food, even if we can't have sauerkraut," Gramps says while looking over at Mae Lee, who responds by threatening to tickle him some more.

Soon all the "necessary items" are packed in the truck along with the jolly sailors. Happy chatter fills the two-seated cab as plans are discussed along the way. Gramma says, "We need to make sure Mae Lee gets a chance to spend time with me watching and naming birds, and the guys need to have more instruction time on how to help Gramps operate the ship."

"While we're driving, Gramps or Gramma, can you tell us why you named your ship *Rainbow's End*?" Sam queries.

"It seems like a strange title because real rainbows don't have an end. You know from an airplane, looking down at a rainbow, it's a complete circle?" Gramps asks.

"Yes, but when looking at a rainbow from ground level, it appears that there are ends," Gramma replies.

"There are other reasons. Think about where rainbows are first mentioned in the Bible, name a few, and let's talk about their meanings," suggests Gramps.

"I know the first one: the rainbow promise of no more world-wide floods in Noah's time," answers Mae Lee.

Sam adds, "I read of a rainbow around God's throne."

"Also, in Revelation, there is a rainbow over Jesus' head," contributes Dave.

"Well, remember kids, so what do all those verses have common in meaning?" continues Gramps.

Sam says, "They all might be telling about God's love and power to save us."

"Those were kind of our thoughts when we came up with that name. God controls the wind and the waves and moves us along to our desired harbor. Gramma and I dedicated this ship to doing God's service and look forward to one day traveling on our wings of wind given us by our Heavenly Father. *'What a day that will be, When my Jesus I shall see, And I look upon His face, The One who saved me by His grace; When He takes me by the hand, And leads me through the Promised Land, What a day, glorious day that will be.'*" Gramps ends by singing.

> *« Gramma and I dedicated this ship to doing God's service and look forward to one day traveling on our wings of wind given us by our Heavenly Father. »*

While the crew of Rainbow's End silently sits, thinking about the words, Gramps arrives at the docking area to unload their tack to transport on their dingy to the ship.

When everything and everyone is finally on board, all scramble to set the ship aright for a day skimming the surface of the azure blue waters of Buzzards Bay towards the open sea. With the wind filling the sails and tangling any stray hair not confined under a hat, the crew gazes into the horizon anticipating what lay ahead. Suddenly, Sam remembers his musical composition and belts it out for all to hear, "Today's the day! We sail the Bay! Whoop, whoop, hurray! Up, up, away!" The waves seem to hear the joy-filled ditty and dance with the music.

After sailing several nautical miles, the wind wanes and the sails lose their tautness. Gramps decides to head over to an island that would be good for bird watching before the ship is becalmed. After they weigh anchor and help Gramma and Mae Lee into the dinghy for their bird watching excursion together, Gramps gives the guys lessons in managing the sails for successful trips, especially under heavy sea when educated quick action is necessary to stay afloat.

With bird book in hand along with a pair of binoculars, Gramma guides Mae Lee to a little shaded spot between a few large rocks and a clump of wind stunted trees clinging tenaciously to what little mossy ground that remains. "We'll sit quietly for a while until the birds get used to us being here and return. Then I'll try to pick out the different species of birds with the binoculars and tell you what name to write down on your pad. After that hopefully, you will get a chance to identify them, too," Gramma suggests. "Names like Northern Gannet, Double-crested Cormorant, Sanderlings, Great Black-backed Gull, Herring Gull, Common Loon, Laughing Gull, Northern Folmar, Shearwater, Common Tern, and White-winged Scoter."

Time passes quickly with everyone busy and the sun gets past noontime when Gramma says, "I was really hoping to see a Roseate Tern because the Buzzards Bay area is their major breeding grounds, but no, guess they're nesting somewhere else. I think, we'd better get back to the ship and eat some lunch with the guys. I'm sure the crew is hungry."

"I'm part of the crew, and I know I'm starved," Mae Lee agrees. Once back aboard, lunch is soon served inside the cabin to keep the seagulls from begging for food while the family is eating. No one wants an unwelcomed addition to a prized sandwich.

While eating, Gramps comes up with a question for consideration, "Since we're still becalmed here, I have some stories I'd like to share. Let's go topside and get comfortable where you can watch the waves ebb and tide." The light breeze, being cooling enough to counteract the heat from the sun, gives all the sensation of it being the most perfect afternoon ever to be floating on the Bay. "Once I find my notes, I have another Longfellow poem for you—okay, found it."

The Secret of the Sea
by Henry Wadsworth Longfellow 1850

(short version)

Ah! what pleasant visions haunt me
As I gaze upon the sea!
All the old romantic legends,
All my dreams, come back to me.

Sails of silk and ropes of sandal,
Such as gleam in ancient lore;
And the singing of the sailors,
And the answer from the shore!

"Wouldst thou,"—so the helmsman answered,
"Learn the secret of the sea?
Only those who brave its dangers
Comprehend its mystery!"

In each sail that skims the horizon,
In each landward-blowing breeze,
I behold that stately galley,
Hear those mournful melodies;

Till my soul is full of longing
For the secret of the sea,
And the heart of the great ocean
Sends a thrilling pulse through me.

"What you are experiencing here today, along with the thoughts like this poem, are probably the reasons that Joseph Bates, at the age of about you fellows, decided he was not going to further his education, but instead become a lowly cabin boy on a ship going across the Atlantic Ocean with no certainty that he might ever return. His father, another Joseph Bates, had spent time and money in establishing the New Bedford Academy, soon after renamed Fairhaven Academy. The school was built in 1798 and nine years later, our Joseph Bates left it for a life on the open sea. Dave, would you please tell the others what you've read about that decision? How did it affect Bates' life?" Gramps inquires.

Dave contemplates his answer for a little while and then answers, "I don't really know whether it was an all bad decision. Maybe so though because he was mistreated, imprisoned, deprived of his rights as an American citizen, tortured because he wouldn't comply with unjust orders, and almost lost his life more than once. However, God did protect him, maybe because He saw something Bates could do for the gospel's sake that most people wouldn't have even attempted. Bates learned skills, knowledge of the sea, and how to survive when all looked lost, his life was amazing. But, overall, I think it would have been best if Bates had continued his schooling longer and matured more before leaving home alone."

"Since we have time while waiting for the wind to pick up more, I'm going to tell you a little about another well-known person who spent quite a bit of time in Fairhaven. Matter of fact, if you wish, sometime, I'll take you on a short walk to his memorial," Gramps continues. "Captain Joshua Slocum was born in 1844, in Annapolis County, Nova Scotia, ran away at the age of fourteen to be a cook on a fishing schooner, but returned home. He left home for good at sixteen when his mother died. At one time, Slocum stayed in the Franklin Bates House next door to the Bates' Boyhood Home while he rebuilt the *Spray* in the area beside it. He departed from Boston Harbor, Massachusetts, on his famous world circumnavigation in 1895, at the age of fifty-one, in the rebuilt thirty-seven-foot sloop *Spray*. He returned, sailing into Newport, Rhode Island, in 1898, a trip of 46,000 miles. To record his adventures, he wrote

Sailing Alone Around the World. It became an instant best seller and you can still buy it today."

"It looks like the wind is picking up," Sam points out. "Shouldn't we be thinking about sailing again?"

"Very observant, Sam ... let's get everything ready to set sail," replies Gramps with a grin. Soon they are up and running with the wind back towards port. After preparing the ship to leave, ferrying their belongs to port-side, and storing them in their truck, the crew heads back to Captain Joseph Bates' Boyhood Home.

After a light supper and clean up, there was time for Mae Lee to go over to Miss Mabel's house to get Lucy and her belongings, before evening worship. When Mae Lee knocks on her back door, Mabel seems a little sad when she hands Lucy over to her. Mae Lee decides to ask, "Was Lucy a good girl while I was gone?"

With a rare, pleased smile, Auntie Mabel responds, "She was a darling, listened to all my troubles without getting tired of them, in her own little cat way talked to me about her wants and wishes, she never gave me any difficulty about putting on her leash harness, and was pleasant company in the evening. She gets a grade of A++! When you have to leave, will you be taking her with you, giving her to your Gramma, or to Patsy to be returned to the shelter?"

《 *If she has to go back to the shelter, please let me know—maybe there is some way I could arrange to keep her.* 》

Mae Lee pauses in thought. This was the first time she really has considered what comes next for Lucy, "I don't know yet—I have to talk to Gramma."

Mabel nods her head and offers the thought, "If she has to go back to the shelter, please let me know—maybe there is some way I could arrange to keep her. Probably, the shelter has to be paid, then there's the cat food and kitty litter. I'd have to figure how I could manage that on my monthly income, but I sure wouldn't want to see her sitting all alone in the shelter for who knows how long." Reaching into an apron pocket and pulling out a crumpled hankie, Mabel dabs her eyes and nose before slowly closing the door.

Burdened with the sadness of the conversation, Mae Lee has difficulty enjoying Lucy's bouncy companionship. As soon as she arrives back to Gramma, Mae Lee tells her of what Mabel said and did. "Well, Mae Lee, what do you want to happen to Lucy?"

"I don't know, now. At first, I wanted to take her with me, but I already have pets at my home and am not sure how they would get along with Lucy. Gramma, would you pray with me about this because there are too many possible sad endings to this story and I really want a happy one?"

"Of course, Mae Lee, let's go in by the couch—the rug is more comfortable than the hard kitchen floor."

After their time in prayer, Mae Lee goes to her room to think. As evening shadows darken the lawn, the family, exhausted from another super busy day, decides that an early bedtime is in order. Quietness settles in like a warm blanket through the house, but for a long while sleep does not come to the little girl with the green-eyed, black cat cuddled up beside her.

CHAPTER TEN

WITH TUESDAY BEING a day on the job, all are up and at 'em early. Dave and Sam offer to fix breakfast together, giving Gramma and Gramps time to check with the volunteer docents about just what's been happening at the Bates' Home these last two days. Mae Lee is slower in coming downstairs, rubbing her eyes, because it was a difficult night of too much thinking and not enough sleeping for her. After feeding Lucy, she ambles outside with the green-eyed feline to think some more. Sunlight and bay mist blend and swirl around the pair bringing peace and an inspirational thought. Finally, Mae Lee looks up through the trees and smiles at the blue sky.

With morning tasks done, and an interesting creative breakfast of caramelized fried toast served with apple slices and hot dogs, the family gather in the living room for worship. Mae Lee quickly announces, "Gramma, I think God told me what to do about Lucy this morning that makes me happy." A room full of silence answers the pronouncement with all anticipating an interesting explanation to follow. With a calm certainty, Mae Lee reveals the plan, "Lucy needs a home, Auntie Mabel needs a companion, and I need to spend the money in my gift red envelope that my Chinese friends gave me. It all fits together you see. Would you please call Patsy and ask her how much a Senior Citizen would have to pay for a pet from the shelter? Then I will know if my money will be enough to pay for that and help Auntie Mabel with buying food and litter for Lucy for at

least a year. By then, I'll have more money saved up from doing jobs at home to give in the future to support Lucy. That way she could kind of stay being my pet because I'm supporting her, and I could come back and visit her sometimes. There is one problem—I know that Auntie Mabel is getting older all the time, and that there may come a time she can no longer take care of Lucy. If that happens, Gramma, would you make sure you get her until I can take her?"

After a pause of shocked but pleased surprise, cheers erupt, amazing the announcer of the applauded plans. Sam, the first to find his voice, yells, "Hip-hip-hurrah! Three cheers for the young lady with the black cat!" After all join in with the requested accolades, Gramma hurries to the phone to check out the possibilities with Patsy. All wait with somewhat bated breath until Gramma waves an OK signal. Then there is dancing in the living room, into the kitchen, and back. When Mae Lee can finally control her laughing, she asks for the costs figures, and receives a "no problem, don't worry" answer from Gramma. "Patsy will come over to figure it all out."

"Okay, we all need to try to remain calm now! No more shouting, stomping, and celebrating, we must get on with our day," Gramps announces with a false solemnity. When all appears quiet, Gramma looks at Gramps with a very sober straight face. The next second, Gramps starts laughing, and Sam and Dave start repeating the dancing and marching around the breakfast table with Mae Lee joining in with Bagel balanced on her head.

When all are finally exhausted, Gramps asks Mae Lee if she would get a New Living Translation Bible and read Luke 6:38. Mae Lee starts to read, "Give, and you will receive. Your gift will return to you in full—pressed down, shaken together to make room for more, running over, and poured into your lap. The amount you give will determine the amount you get back."

"What do you think this means, Mae Lee?" Gramps asks.

"Well, maybe it means that when we help others, we are helped ourselves," she responds.

"My thoughts exactly!" Gramps continues. "This illustrates another story in the life of Joseph Bates that I want to share this morning. Joseph was totally dedicated to spreading the Adventist message. He not only worked with no salary, but gave generously from his own money. By the time of the mid-1840s he had donated his whole retirement funds of about $10,000, which today would maybe be equivalent to about $300,000. He didn't think he needed the money for retiring because Jesus was coming very soon. In 1849, James White wrote this about Bates, 'He was an outcast, and has spent all his property in the Holy Advent cause. Yet he is rich, yes, glory to God, he is a rich servant of Jesus Christ. But few know of his trials, labors, sufferings in the cause of present truth, in which he devotes his whole time.' James and Ellen lent a home for Joseph and Prudy to live in for fourteen months and refused to accept rent.

"One time, Bates wanted to travel to do a preaching tour, but he didn't have any money. After praying about it, God impressed him to just get on the train. He had been seated for only a few moments when a stranger walked up and handed him the five dollars that was needed for his ticket. Another time the Allegan and Monteray Churches of Michigan gave him $12 (about $300 in today's money economy), so that he could buy a coat. Listen to Bates' attitude towards money in this statement of his: 'All my poor services and a thousand times more could never pay the purchase of my redemption. I want to remain in his service while I continue in this mortal state.'"

Gramps finishes, "It just shows, I think that we are most rich when we are the most generous. Let's finish worship with prayer. Dear Lord, giver of all that we possess, we pray that You help us to emulate Your gracious spirit of generosity. We pray for all the people who are now involved in spreading the good news of Your redemption and Your soon coming, especially we remember our son and daughter-in-law. Please keep them from harm while in that foreign land and bring them home safely. Watch over us today, please, and keep us in Your service. In Christ's name we pray, Amen."

"Some good news I want to share with you," Gramps enthusiastically announces, "but I'm not going say all of it!"

"Why, Gramps why?" Mae Lee says. "Are you just teasing me again?"

Putting up a hand to stop her progress, Gramps adds, "Before you attack with your tickling fingers, I must explain. Your parents will be in a place where they can go live on the Internet and we'll be able to talk with them, almost face to face, this early evening." Immediately, a loud cheer erupts. "Okay, I'm glad you're happy—Gramma and I certainly are, too. The day will go by more quickly if we all get busy. I need to point out that today and tomorrow are the last days you have to work on your reports. We'd like to have you present your reports tomorrow evening right after supper. Can you manage that?" After the kids look at each other, and nod yes. Gramps continues, "Okay, good! Gramma and I will be busy in the visitor center and the Bates' Home. We never know when visitors might arrive unexpectedly. Please stay at the house, but you can find us if anything comes up for which you need help. We'll be back to get lunch ready about noon." After Mae Lee jumps up and runs upstairs carrying Bagel, Gramps motions the boys to come over closer to him and says, "Please keep track of what Mae Lee is doing to make sure that she is safe and that her imagination doesn't carry her away somewhere we can't find her, alright?"

"We'll take turns being her watch dog ... don't worry Gramps," Dave answers.

Sam says, "Trust us—we know just what to do." With that assurance, Gramps sighs a little and walks out locking the door behind him.

The morning's academic study was progressing quietly. After an hour, Dave checks in on Mae Lee, converses a little about her project, and leaves feeling all is going well. An hour later, it is Sam's turn for a check in. This time there is no girl in the small bedroom. Lucy the cat is there sleeping on the bed next to Bagel, but no one else. However, the noise of the nearby road construction coming in through the open window is so annoying, that Sam shuts it and starts off looking other places in the house. Unsuccessful at that, he checks the outside door in the kitchen and finds that it is still locked! Surprised and now a little concerned, Sam starts yelling, "Okay, Mae Lee, the hide and seek game is over, you win, where are you?"

The only response that can be heard is Dave yelling, "You lost Mae Lee?"

Sam replies, "I didn't lose her—I can't find her! We've got a problem here. I'm going over to get our grandparents."

"I'll stay here and keep looking," adds Dave.

Soon Gramps, Gramma, and Sam come running in and together ask, "You find her?"

"No! I'm getting really annoyed if you're still hiding Mae Lee—out with you!" Dave's command is answered with silence in the home except for the grinding roadwork noise from outside.

"Okay, Gramma, why don't you check with the neighbors to see if any of them have seen her; I'll go check out the Bates' Home again to see if she's there; Dave stay here and call us on our cell phones if she shows up while we're gone; and Sam, scout out our neighborhood further away look behind bushes, trees, and such. Everybody needs to meet back here when you're done," commands Gramps. A half hour goes by before all the searchers return empty handed and with concern written all over their faces.

"We'd better call the police," Gramma anxiously suggests.

"Let's pray about it first … should have done that before we went out looking," Gramps agonizes and prays, "Dear Lord, God of wisdom and all knowledge, please safely return Mae Lee to us, or help us find her. Thank You for listening. We know that You love her even more than we do. Amen."

Just at the moment, there is a knock at the door, all dash to open it with happy expectation, only to find that it is Miss Mabel. "I know, you were hoping that it would be Mae Lee knocking and are disappointed, but I'm been thinking about her disappearance and have some questions that might answer where she is now," she says and then asks, "When you went into her bedroom were Lucy and Bagel there?"

Sam thinks about it for a second and replies, "Yes, both were there as if nothing strange was going on."

"That's what is strange! Mae Lee never would have left them there unless she was planning to return soon. I suggest we go back to her room and look for more clues," adds Miss Mabel.

Quickly, all rush to the scene of the suspected crime and start looking around. "Be careful, don't disturb anything, we may be calling the police soon," commands Gramma.

Lucy had moved from the bed onto the windowsill and started to furiously scratch on the glass. "Not now, Lucy, you don't go out that window anyways," Dave says.

All of a sudden a thought strikes Sam, "The window! The window had been open!"

Rushing to it, he slides open the window and looks out. It was only then that the voice of a little girl is heard above the noise of the roadwork, "I'm too afraid to climb down. Help me!" Sam quickly climbs out, much to his grandparents' surprise and alarm, and starts to climb the iron fire escape ladder attached to the side of the house. Soon he is back at the window with Mae Lee clinging to him. Handing her over first, Sam safely works his own larger body inside through the window's opening. Tears of joy mix with relief as all collapse onto Mae Lee's bed or hug the former damsel in distress.

Mae Lee speaks first accusingly, "How come you shut the window? I couldn't get back in and I couldn't make you hear me no matter how loud I shouted!"

Sam replies, "Why would I ever have thought you had climbed out it? You never have done that before!" All wait with expectation for some kind of logical response.

"I needed to do a little more study on the life of seagulls for my report and decided to get out where I could see them better," Mae Lee explains. Her response is almost as astounding as her rescue and so no one can think of a comeback statement for a long while.

With all the excitement over, life returns to a normal pace. Gramps and Gramma finish up some work at the museum and the "authors" work on their projects until lunch time. When all are involved in getting the meal together, another knock is heard. Gramma and Mae Lee open the door to find Patsy there. She explains, "I'm playing hookie during my lunch time from the animal shelter. Justa save time while I'm in the neighborhood, thought I'd fix up the switcheroo for Lucy to belong to your Auntie Mabel. Hey, I do this, not for nuthin, but let me tell ya, I enjoy seeing pets go to good homes. Jeet? You wouldn't have an extra grinda I could snack on while I tell ya what we can do 'bout this."

Gramma quickly interprets what was said and offers the desired food. Once seated with a quick lunch in front of her, Patsy continues, "Sorry to hurry ya so, my caah might be in the way out there, if we hear some honken I'll have to leave before a cruiser shows up and I get an undesirable caad. OK, this is how I sees it. Mae Lee is goin' to finance this whole shebang with Chinese money, is that right?"

"Almost, but not quite—it's American money that people from China gave her. You'll just have to see this beautifully designed envelope that contains the money! Mae Lee would you go get it, please?" Gramma requests. While Mae Lee is gone, Gramma quickly explains the plan Mae Lee has of working to buy a continuing supply of food and litter for Lucy. "We will help with that need if necessary, so please don't upset Mae Lee by questioning her ability to raise the money. Just take whatever the cat adoption fee is for the shelter and we'll handle the rest," Gramma ends quickly.

"Great idear! Mums the waud, I get it. Smaaht of ya," Patsy says with a wink as Mae Lee walks in the room.

"Is this enough money, Patsy?" Mae Lee asks as she hands her the bright red envelope.

Patsy looks in it and gives a loud whistle, "It all depends if you wanta pay off my college loan, plus the cat or not. Plenty heah, and enough to support Lucy into her old age. Not to worry! Heh, because Mabel is a member of the senior's club, so ta speak, she gets to pay nexta nutin'. I'll take out what's needed, you hang on the rest. Tell me, kid, when ya leavin? I wanna get over one last time and see how everythin' is with ya. You alls a great bunch of people. Gotta go!" Patsy talks as she's walking out the door.

"Come Friday morning before you start work at the animal shelter; we'll be up," Gramma shouts as Patsy is halfway to her car.

Gramps sums up everyone's thoughts about Patsy, "She comes and goes like a summer storm, leaving flowers blooming more brightly."

The rest of the day seems to drag for the family. Each is wanting the promised phone call to come through soon. After a light supper, Gramps calls everyone in for an early worship time. "Dave, would you turn to Luke 15:4–7 and read it?" Gramps asks.

"Here it is: 'Suppose one of you has a hundred sheep and loses one of them. Doesn't he leave the ninety-nine in the open country and go after the lost sheep until he finds it? And when he finds it, he joyfully puts it on his shoulders and goes home. Then he calls his friends and neighbors together and says, 'Rejoice with me; I have found my lost sheep.' I tell you that in the same way there will be more rejoicing in heaven over one sinner who repents than over ninety-nine righteous persons who do not need to repent."

Dave continues, "We all know why you chose that verse!" looking over at Mae Lee, who responds with "why me?" look.

"It's more than that Dave," Gramps adds. "It's linked with a very personal and painful experience that both Joseph and Prudy Bates experienced on the day before October 22, 1844. Remember, that was when the people in the Millcrite movement believed that Jesus was going to come and take His redeemed ones home. Their son, Joseph, left that day for a life of working at sea. It broke their hearts that their son had not accepted Christ as a personal friend and to their understanding he would be lost to God's kingdom of grace and they would never see him again. Son, Joseph, later became a whaler and was lost at sea at the age of thirty-five. After Captain Bates' became a follower of Jesus, he tirelessly worked to save the spiritually lost. The last home Bates lived in was near Monterey, Michigan. If you ever get up that way with your parents, be sure to go to the little white Adventist church in Allegan, Michigan. Bates designed its construction patterned after a ship, only this one would be considered bottom side up with the keel on top. At this church is also a pulpit that Ellen White designed and Joseph built. Something else important started at Allegan: *The Morning Star* boat, herald of the Adventist message to the South, was put together and launched there. The gospel ministry was Joseph's burning passion until the time of his death in 1872. His and Prudy's gravesite, a ways north of there, is in the Poplar Hill Cemetery. Bates was a lifelong seeker of the lost. Like your parents now on a mission trip on the other side of the world, at the Joseph Bates' Home, we also have the privilege of introducing people to the saving grace of Jesus by telling the stories of Adventist history."

Worship is interrupted by the beeping of Gramma's tablet signaling an incoming video call. Mae Lee shouts, "It's them! I know it's Mom and Dad!"

Gramma runs and gets it open and ready for all to see and to be seen. "Oh, my, so good to see you! How's the evangelistic series going?" Gramma asks.

"It just ended with a baptism of several precious people today. We'll be leaving tomorrow to come home, the Internet is not too good here, we might be cut off anytime, but we so need to see our children," Mom and Dad both say as they crowd onto the screen. Mae Lee grabs the tablet and kisses it over and over saying, "I miss you so" between kisses. With everyone laughing, the tablet finally gets arranged back again where everyone can see through the smooched glass. "Before we get cut off, we have to tell you something. We are celebrating! Word has just come that Mae Lee's and Sam's adoption is final and we now are officially your parents!" Mom and Dad announce with a shout of joy. This is followed by whoops, more shouts of joy, a small dark-haired girl bouncing up and down, and everyone hugging.

"This is the happiest day of my life!" Mae Lee proclaims.

"I am filled with such ecstatic ecstasy that it eclipses the epitome of any my previous hereto for euphoric experiences!" enunciates Sam. The parents, laughing and smiling as broadly as any tablet can reproduce, start saying, "I love …" when the signal is lost.

After a moment of silence, Dave says, "I want to officially hug my brother and sister!" While holding them close he continues, "This is a new beginning for me. I've never had a brother and sister before. I just want to say I love you and want to be the best older brother possible. Please forgive me for any of my mistakes in the past. This is a new beginning for us all. Know that I will always be there for you when you need help or just a friend to listen." Tears of joy turn to tears of warm sentimental feelings.

"I hate to ruin the party, but it's been quite the day! We need to tend to some items at the museum. Would you all please go over there with us? We treasure your company especially now that we officially belong together," Gramps states.

"Can I get Lucy on her leash and walk her along; she hasn't been out all day?" Mae Lee requests. After getting consent, Mae Lee goes into action. All is quiet outside now and the sun's setting rays warm the air and the people walking in its quiet light. Even Miss Mabel is outside tending to her small flower garden.

Seeing her, Mae Lee, walking as fast at Lucy is able to keep up, approaches with the intent of sharing the news about the finalized adoption, when Mabel speaks the first words, "So I suppose you're leaving with my kitty friend, right soon?"

"You're partly right, our plane leaves Friday, but Lucy isn't going with me," Mae Lee answers.

Looking a little like her old stern self, with a deep frown, Mabel accuses, "So you're returning our 'baby' to the shelter!"

《 This is a new beginning for me. I've never had a brother and sister before. I just want to say I love you and want to be the best older brother possible. 》

Almost enjoying this repartee, Mae Lee says, "No, she's staying here with you, if you still want her."

"It's not whether I want her or not, it's just that ... I can't afford her," Mabel says with tears in her voice.

Mae Lee replies in a laughing voice, "You don't need to afford anything—I've already arranged it with Patsy and Gramma. Everything, and I mean everything, has been paid for. Lucy is yours as a totally free gift. You just need to love her. You will love Lucy, right?" Mae Lee questions.

This statement is followed by an amazed gasp of joy, as Mabel asks, "She's mine to keep … forever?"

In answer, Mae Lee shakes her head and body up and down, "I'll give her and all her stuff to you Friday morning before I leave."

"It's hard to believe, Mae Lee; thank you so much. How can I ever thank you enough? You've made my somber life full of hope and sunshine!" Mabel beams.

"You're very welcome," Mae Lee says as she gives Auntie Mabel a hug, "I've got to go now, they're waiting for me at the museum and they no longer want to go hunting for me. Bye, see you later."

With the kids helping, several clean up jobs, and other museum errands are done quickly, and the family walk slowly through the gathering dusk with fireflies lighting the way, back to the house. Once inside, Gramps says, "We've already had worship, but need to offer prayer before going to our rooms for the night."

Mae Lee asks if she can offer the prayer and then begins, "Dear Father of light and happiness, You have given us so much joy today, my heart is so full that it almost feels like it's going to pop wide open. Thank you that Sam and I have a really truly Mom and Dad forever and ever. I pray, that someday, when You come in the clouds, I will see my mother in heaven because I love her, too. Thank you for giving us Jesus and that we didn't have to pay for Him. He came free as a gift from the goodness of your heart. Please watch over us all as we sleep tonight. I love You so much. Amen."

CHAPTER ELEVEN

THE STEADY, SOFT patter of raindrops on the windowsill perform a soft lullaby. The sleeper knows not when morning breaks because the sound of its shattered pieces fall too far away to reach her ears. However, the one creature of the home that sleeps intermittently, day and night, wants everyone awake, and now! Her stomach's alarm clock had sounded and could only be quieted with crunchy kitty morsels. Mae Lee awakes with Lucy's wet nose touching hers. "Oh, so you think I've slept long enough, do you? Okay, I get up. Only three more days and then you go to Auntie Mabel's. I miss you already! Rainy days make me sad."

"That reminds me of Longfellow again," Gramps adds from the doorway. "I think it goes like this: *'And the days are dark and dreary. Be still, sad heart, and cease repining; Behind the clouds is the sun still shining; Thy fate is the common fate of all, Into each life some rain must fall, Some days must be dark and dreary.'*

"With a full stomach, you both will feel better about the day. We have breakfast ready, sleepyhead. Come when you can!" Gramps calls over his shoulder as he heads back in the direction from which the inviting aromas originate.

When breakfast is over, discussion revolves around plans for the day. Gramma announces, "We have visitors coming this morning. They told me that they are crossing the country seeing all the Adventist Heritage sites along the way. They've been to the Historic Adventist Village in Battle Creek, Michigan; the Hiram Edson Farm near Clifton Springs, New York; and then the William Miller Farm at Whitehall, New York. We're the last one in this section of the country. It will be interesting to hear of their travels. The great Advent movement never stops!"

Dave observes, "Gramps you told us about Joseph Bates going to Michigan and the William Miller Farm, but did he also go to Hiram Edson's Farm?"

"Oh, yes, he was there more than once. Bates even went on preaching tours with Edson in the winter where they had to end up walking in deep cold snow for miles. They wanted to carry the truth about the good news of the judgment and the Sabbath to remote towns and homes of Advent believers near the Lake Ontario region of upstate New York. I even have an almost funny story about Bates that I'll tell you for worship. Let's put breakfast things away and have worship," Gramps suggests.

"Sam, please get a Bible and look up 2 Timothy 4:1, 2. This is where Paul is telling his young intern Timothy, how to spread the gospel."

"Sure Gramps, here it is: *'I give you this charge: Preach the word; be prepared in season and out of*

season; correct, rebuke and encourage—with great patience and careful instruction.'"

"Sam could you give us an illustration on how a person is supposed to do that?"

"I'm thinking back to when we met Patsy at the Phoenix Park. You told the story of Bates and the Sabbath right there, even though I don't think you were planning on doing that, right?" Sam offers. When Gramps nods assent Sam continues, "So then, 'In season' could mean when someone asks you to do it and 'out of season' might mean that you do it unplanned by you, but it's God-planned."

Gramps responds, "Wonderful job, Sam. Now on with our story for today. In 1846, probably late in the year, Bates made a trip out to see Edson after he had read Edson's understanding of the beginning of the judgment in 1844. Bates had another reason to meet Edson: he wanted to share the little book that he had written about the true Sabbath, which Edson accepted. Later in August of 1848, Bates came back to the Edson's farm for a Biblical study meeting that the Whites and other leaders attended to study into all the different aspects of what was truth as presented in scripture. After the meeting, James and Ellen White, along with Bates, went to arrange a trip to New York City by boat traveling the Erie Canal. The only one they could get at that time was a slow-moving boat that made a lot of stops along the way. So they paid their fare and got on, hoping that they later could switch to a faster one. Sure enough, after a while one was catching up to them, but didn't want to slow down to a stop for them to transfer over. It just slowed down some. The plan was for those wanting to transfer, to just jump from one boat to the other and pay later. So James got ready by picking up Ellen to jump with her in his arms. Maybe that's what distracted Bates because when Bates went to jump, he

> « 'In season' could mean when someone asks you to do it and 'out of season' might mean that you do it unplanned by you, but it's God-planned. »

misjudged about how high his jump had to be to make it safely on board. When his foot hit the side of this faster boat, his whole body dropped into the canal. While holding the fare for the three of them, yelling to the captain, 'Here! Here, take your pay!' he missed the boat. He surfaced treading water, still with his pocketbook in one hand and the dollar in the other. Then he had a dilemma—he had to choose between losing his floating hat versus keeping the dollar bill. The hat won out. Joseph had sailed the world as a captain of his own ship, now here he had the embarrassment of falling off a boat. The passengers fished him out of the water. Fortunately, the day was warm and at a later stop in Centerport, New York, the three disembarked for a drying time at the home of Mr. and Mrs. Harris.

"The next day, they continued their journey. However, while at their home, James, Ellen, and Joseph had time to share the Advent message with the Harris family. They later became believers and joined the Sabbath-keeping Adventist. That maybe is an example of sharing 'out of season.' So, I think we must be always aware that God's planned divine appointments can pop up any time and any place."

"Yes, a serendipitous situation, I would think," Sam adds.

After all quizzically stare at Sam for a while, Gramps continues, "Sam, using your newly-acquired gift of somewhat foreign sounding words to us, would you please close worship with a prayer?"

Nodding his head, Sam intones the words, "Dear Lord, mighty Creator of the Universe, Sustainer of galaxies, please look down and direct our paths today in keeping with Your will. Thank You for hearing and answering this petition, Amen."

After another pause, Gramps asks, "Sam, where have you been getting these astounding words?"

"Reading, Gramps, just reading. I promise not to put long words in my report though—I wouldn't want to make it too difficult for you to understand," Sam replies, laughing as he starts dodging pillows being thrown at him.

The day turns out to be productive for the kids as they prepare their reports for their evening's entertainment and educational presentations.

Artwork and photos are being pulled together to illustrate their concepts. Time moves by quickly. Then the kids become aware of a truck arriving, pulling a family-size camper. After it pulls in, they watch the occupants looking around the grounds for the best spot. Dave calls Gramma, "The family is here that you were expecting. Did you give them permission to camp here?"

Gramma replies, "Yes, but only for the night, then they're traveling on tomorrow morning early. The camper is self-contained, so they won't have to use our facilities."

"I was wondering if it would be okay for us to go out to greet them and lend them a helping hand if we could?" Dave adds.

"Sure, and then send them on to the museum and get back to your projects. If you, Sam, and Mae Lee would like, I suggest that you ask the family if they want to hear you project reports this evening after supper."

Dave replies, "I'll see what the others think. Bye for now."

Mae Lee says, "Let's go, I'd like to meet them." Sam is already partway out the door and is the first one to greet the visitors. After introductions, the kids help the family find an appropriate level area, set up their campsite, offer the visitors prime seats to hear their evening's presentations, and point out the best way to get into the museum.

Returning to the house, Sam asks, "Did you hear them say that they are a homeschool family and that this trip is part of their curriculum? Imagine a school where you learn as you travel. Sounds like fun!"

Dave replies, "Their license plate shows they're from Alaska! What a trip that must be! Think of all the places you could visit. We'd better move right along on our jobs, so we can spend more time with the family, later."

"Sounds good to me!" Sam adds.

"Oh, I guess so," says Mae Lee apprehensively.

"What's wrong, Mae Lee, you scared?" questions Sam. "Do you remember how you did that whole big group of Chinese visitors? You did great!"

Looking down, Mae Lee says, "That was speaking in Chinese, maybe my English is not so good."

"Hey, not to worry, I'll interpret your English into my English and then all will be Supercalifragilisticexpialidocious!" Sam offers.

"No, you won't, they will be giggling all the way through," Mae Lee laughingly replies. "Put those pillows down, Mae Lee ... flying projectiles do not intimidate me in the least! Okay, jokes over! I've got to get going on it." Sam ends the conversation and leaves.

Mae Lee stands there for a while with two pillows in her hands and asking no one in particular, "What did he say?"

After the museum's closing time, Gramma and Gramps return to find the kids already getting supper together. Gramps looks around at what's cooking and asks, "What no sauerkraut?"

"Saving it for your breakfast," Sam replies with a wink.

After eating the soup and sandwiches that were created, Gramma observes, "That was a unique soup. Can you share the list of ingredients with me?"

Dave replies, "I don't know for sure what they were, Mae Lee had already taken off the labels for recycling before I opened them. Sam, you picked the cans out, what were they?"

"I don't know, just the first five containers I found in the front of the cupboard, plus a box of soup base liquid or was it soap based? 'All's well that ends well' is what I always say," Sam offers.

Gramps questions Gramma, "Do you have the phone number for poison control handy, just in case we need it this evening?" Laughing, the kids admit that they hadn't made it at all, but that their visitors had offered them part of their supper's soup. Mae Lee ends by observing that she thought the soup was simply Supercalifragilisticexpialidocious! Gramma looks at Gramps and questions, "Do you think it's contagious?"

After supper, their guests arrive and are ushered into seats in the living room. Mae Lee walks in holding a sign made of poster board with the words: "Part one: **Birds of a feather, sometimes fight together: Seagulls 101.**" Placing the sign on a table next to Bagel and her notes, she clears her throat dramatically and begins. "When visitors come to the Joseph Bates Home they need to get to know one of the most interesting of God's creatures that live here, the Seagulls of Buzzards Bay!" Sam starts clapping. Mae Lee stops and stares at him and shakes her head with a bemused frown. Beginning again, Mae Lee starts, "Seagulls are fun to watch and feed. There are many types of seagulls here. I'll name a few you can find here: the Herring, Ring-Billed, Laughing, Little, Black-Headed, Bonaparte's, Iceland, Lesser Black-backed, Glaucous, Greater Black-backed, and sometimes the Sabine's. Seagulls usually live about fifteen years, but when they are kept protected they can live forty-nine years. They eat both plants and animals and are very smart about it. They have the talent to see ultraviolet light and have excellent eyesight, even when it is quite dark outside which helps them find food easily.

"When soaring high in the air, they have been seen dropping mussels onto rocks to crack them. Other foods they like are crabs, mussels, and small fish, but they will eat your food if you take it to them and throw it into the air. They think it is a game and try to catch as much as they can. Then they fight over it, yelling things, like "mine, mine, mine", at least that's what I think they say. Unlike the song sparrows and the chickadees, seagulls just make loud call sounds to talk to their friends or enemies. They sometimes are very noisy and go after other animals and people in not nice ways, but they are very loyal to their mates and stay together all their lives. They build their nests together on the ground, sand or cliffs and lay about three eggs at a time.

"They come in different sizes, but are mostly white, gray, and black colors and have webbed feet which helps them swim very well. Seagulls are found on every continent, but like to live near water areas, especially near the ocean's coastal waters. They are able to drink both fresh and saltwater. They have very wide wingspans with pointed ends and long, sharp-hooked bills that can open very wide so they can swallow big creatures. Seagulls seem to really like to dive into the water for their food. Once I saw some baby seagulls, they were so cute that I wanted to take one home, but Gramma said it would probably die if I did that. Seagulls will work together to drive their enemies, like eagles and hawks, away. One thing I read that's kind of smart of them, is that they will take their webbed feet and stomp on the ground to make the worms think it's raining. Then the worms come up to the surface and get eaten by the gulls.

"If you ever see a gull standing on only one foot, probably they are warming their legs one at a time under their feathers. Seagulls are beautiful and fun to watch from the top of your house, but be careful if you do that and tell people first. We all need to work together to help them survive, they almost died out in the 1800s. Now, they are protected by the government. Things we can do to help them and all ocean creatures survive is to not put trash in the waterways and oceans. Please try to recycle containers and use less plastic things that end up in the landfills. Do not use plastic straws! Thank you for your kind attention." Looking at Sam, she says, "Now, you may clap!" Others join in with a rounding applause to which Mae Lee politely bows and announces that there will a brief intermission while waiting for the next presentation.

The audience stands, stretches, and chats, while Sam makes a quick exit. After about ten minutes, a strange trumpet blast is heard and Mae Lee announces, "It is time to be seated please, part two will start now." Then she places another poster board card in front of hers that reads, "Part two: **Tall Ships and Tales of America's History**."

> « *Don't look now, but I think Sam has borrowed a lot of things from our closets and kitchen. I hope he doesn't hurt himself trying to walk in my tall high-heeled winter boots.* »

Gramps whispers to Gramma, "That almost sounded like my old trumpet."

She answers, "Don't look now, but I think Sam has borrowed a lot of things from our closets and kitchen. I hope he doesn't hurt himself trying to walk in my tall high-heeled winter boots."

"I do believe that he has on my old suit jacket with the collar and sleeves turned up," Gramps adds.

"My long winter scarf wrapped around his waist looks like a good contrasting accent," comments Gramma, "I hope he doesn't injure himself with that long old dull kitchen knife slid in under the scarf. I wonder whose hat does he have on upside down with one side of the brim pinned up with an old broach of mine?"

"I'm beginning to think the hat once belonged to me, but I'm wondering how he constructed that patch over his right eye, looks very authentic what with the spy glass and his drawn on black mustache he's quite the pirate!" Gramps stops whispering once he sees Sam about to begin his reenactment speech.

"Ahoy, mates, welcome to me ship!" Pulling out his spyglass and extending it, and looking through it around the room, Sam continues, "Shiver me timbers! Looks like we are marooned here together for a fortnight or so. You look like a fine crew of hearties. Man the pumps and stay away from me booty or you'll be walking the plank! Arrrr! Ho-ho-ho, ye weren't fooled by my hard words were ye? In the past some scallywag hornswaggled me out of my last doubloons which I didn't take kindly to. I'm sure you lads and lassies wouldn't do such a dastardly deed to this buccaneer. Arrrr! Time to weigh anchor and get on with this talk.

"Now I'm going to talk about the people who actually lived and worked in New Bedford and Fairhaven, Massachusetts who were not pirates, but privateers. The privateers were actually employed to protect American ports where the tall ships docked. At the beginning of the American Revolution, New Bedford was a large money-making town. Privateers made the New Bedford harbor a base for attacking the British shipping. Because of that, on September 5, 1778, a large force of British troops landed at Clark's Point, marched into town by way of County Street and attacked Bedford Village. They burned many buildings, shipping, wharves and warehouses, destroying large stores of goods on both sides of the river. They killed four men. It took the little village more than a decade to recover. You can go to Phoenix Park, not far from here, where much of this happened. So privateers were captains of merchant ships legally sanctioned to attack and capture ships of enemy nations.

"American privateers played an important role in the American Revolution by attacking British ships. When the United States Constitution was written, it contained a provision for the federal government to hire privateers. In the War of 1812, American privateers helped by attacking or destroying British merchant ships. The American privateers actually did much more damage to British shipping than the U.S. Navy. American privateer captains became heroes during the War of 1812, and their stories were written up in American newspapers. London newspapers called Baltimore a "nest of pirates." The most well-known of the Baltimore privateers was Joshua Barney, a naval hero of the Revolutionary War who volunteered to serve in the summer of 1812 and was hired as a privateer by President James Madison. Barney was very successful at raiding British ships on the open ocean. At one time, he was able to capture 150 tons of coal. After the burning of Washington, D.C., the British wanted to burn Baltimore, too. However, America's defense of the city prevented it from happening. It was at that time, Francis Scott Key wrote the 'The Star-Spangled Banner.' Would you stand and sing the first verse with me?"

> *Oh, say can you see by the dawn's early light*
> *What so proudly we hailed at the twilight's last gleaming?*
> *Whose broad stripes and bright stars through the perilous fight,*
> *O'er the ramparts we watched were so gallantly streaming?*
> *And the rocket's red glare, the bombs bursting in air,*
> *Gave proof through the night that our flag was still there.*
> *Oh, say does that star-spangled banner*
> *yet wave O'er the land of the free and the home of the brave?*

The whole audience breaks into resounding applause with Mae Lee still clapping when everyone else has stopped. Sam bows repeatedly, losing his hat and other parts of his costume each time and announces, "There will be a short break in our program before the final grand finale."

While people are milling around, Mae Lee gets the last placard, "**Joseph Bates: Captain Courageous**." Dave leaves the room quickly, soon returns in a dress suit, places his lap top computer on the small table up front, and solemnly intones, "Would the congregation please be seated for our concluding presentation."

Sam responds, "Whatever you say, professor!" and Mae Lee claps.

Hand gesturing for them to stop and be seated, Dave begins, "Much of what I will be presenting comes from reading various books written on the life of Joseph Bates, plus his own autobiography. I'm not going to focus so much on what he said and did as to what I've come to understand as to why God chose him to be the flagship of our faith as Seventh-day Adventists. He had attributes crucial for that time and place to start this worldwide movement that is still expanding today. Quoting the news article, 'Adventists Fastest-Growing Denomination' by G. Jeffery MacDonald, 'Since the mid-19th century when the movement sprang up in New Hampshire, Seventh-day Adventism has had an urgent mission to bring the gospel—with a distinctive emphasis on Christ's imminent second coming—to the ends of the earth. Adventists find the essence of their mission in Revelation 14:12, where the end of the age calls for patient endurance on the part of the people of God who keep His commands and remain faithful to Jesus.

"I have found Joseph Bates' life story to be almost too exciting to be considered non-fiction. He never walked in the shadow of another, except Christ. He created news as well as delivered it. He was more of an innovator than Steve Jobs. Maybe the only project that he failed at was trying to start a silk industry in Fairhaven, Massachusetts. Even that project wasn't without precedence. Beginning in the 1830s, not far from Fairhaven is Manchester, Connecticut, where the Cheney Brothers, the first in the United States to properly raise them commercially. The mulberry tree was the fad of that decade. Other smaller producers began raising silkworms. This business venture particularly gained success near Northampton, Massachusetts, and its neighboring Williamsburg. Among the most well-known of these was the Northampton Association for Education and Industry, of which Sojourner Truth was a member. How's that for name dropping? At the time Bates began his silk business, he lived at 19 Mulberry Street in Fairhaven where he built his own home, barn, and planted three acres of mulberry trees. He definitely was a hard-working individual.

"Yes, I'm defending Joseph Bates' reputation! However, I guess I can't defend his handwriting skills. I read that his logbook was almost illegible. However, there's probably a lot of geniuses out there going around with the same type of handwriting. He was the Adventist's first theologian, historian, mission theorist, missionary (Canada, northern New England, and Midwestern region of the United States), converter of many of the top names of the church's original leadership, and the denomination's first health reformer. He promoted church organization without which we would still probably just be considered just a small local religious cult.

"Organization eventually resulted in our mission going to almost all the world. We know we're not there yet because Jesus promised, 'And this gospel of the kingdom will be preached in all the world as a witness to all the nations, and then the end will come.' Matthew 24:14. Christ has not come yet! We need every Advent-believing man, woman, boy, and girl to be involved, pushing our limits, out of love for our Lord and King Jesus, just like Joseph Bates. He's one of the first that I want to shake hands with when we reach our heavenly kingdom. In closing, please stand with me and pray the Lord's Prayer together:

> *Our Father, which art in heaven,*
> *Hallowed be thy Name.*
> *Thy Kingdom come.*
> *Thy will be done in earth,*
> *As it is in heaven.*
> *Give us this day our daily bread.*
> *And forgive us our trespasses,*
> *As we forgive them that trespass against us.*
> *And lead us not into temptation,*
> *But deliver us from evil.*
> *For thine is the kingdom,*
> *The power, and the glory,*
> *For ever and ever.*
> *Amen.*

CHAPTER TWELVE

THE NEXT DAY, the sea breeze is up, before the sun, rattling the shutters by the windows. The younger occupants at 191 Main Street, Fairhaven, Massachusetts, are still slumbering when they hear a melody floating through their dreams, gradually getting closer and more distinct, "Over and over, like a mighty sea, comes the love of Jesus rolling over me. Over the sea, over the sea, Jesus Saviour, pilot me. over the sea, over the sea, over the jasper sea."

Sam, first awake, asks, "Gramps, would you sing it again? I'd like to learn that one and sing it out on the open bay, today." As the two start together, Dave's voice joins in.

Gramps calls, "Heh, little miss sleepy head, you're missing out, what about joining us and make it a quartet?"

"I'm too sad," was the only response.

"Why, pray tell?" Gramps questions.

"There's only this day left before we leave and I'm missing you, Gramma, and Lucy already. Really, I'd be happier to just stay by the museum and be with Lucy," Mae Lee answers.

Gramma overhears the conversation as she ascends the stairs and joins in, "Your wish is granted! I just got a phone call from a tour group that we didn't know was coming, asking if they could stop by today even if we normally are not open on Thursdays. I told them that I would be here. So, Mae Lee, if you wish, you can stay at the museum with me."

In the next second, the sleepyhead became a bouncing ball on her bed yelling, "Yes, yes, yes!"

Gramps quips, "Okay, little Miss Mae Lee, get ready for the day!"

"Gramps, you're a poet, and I know it!"

With groans resounding from the brothers, Gramma descends the stairs saying, "Too early in the day! Poetry, go away!"

When all are up and properly attired for the day's events, and breakfast is being consumed rapidly, Gramps goes over the agenda, "Okay, boys, today we sail across Buzzards Bay to Cuttyhunk Island, a small island between here and Martha's Vineyard. The ladies will be staying home today because visitors are coming to the Bates' Home. Perhaps we can share a Bates story or two while we are out sailing. It should be an exciting day. The wind is going to be a bit strong for sailing. So we will plan to go early and get back before late afternoon when things can often get rough out on Buzzards Bay. It's quite a ways to sail in one day, but Jason says he's an expert sailor, so we should be working with good experience." The "crew" boarded the boat in nearly calm conditions in the inner harbor in New Bedford. The inner harbor is the area behind a massive sea wall that was constructed to protect the harbor in the case of a hurricane. Of course, that wall was not there when Joseph used this harbor.

《 *Soon after passing out through the gate in the sea wall, the waves become more boisterous and the wind increases.* 》

All hands help get the boat ready to sail. The sail covers are removed and stowed, the boom is prepared to raise the sail, the winches are uncovered, and winch crank handles placed near where they are needed. Sam stows the lunch in the cabin, and they all slather on some sunscreen.

Gramps announces that they are ready to cast off, and Jason loosens the rope to the mooring and then goes to raise the sail. That involves fastening one end of the halyard to the top corner of the sail and wrapping the other end around the winch at the base of the mast. By cranking the winch and guiding the sail up a slot in the mast, the sail is raised to the top of the mast. Gramps tightens the boom with the block and tackle and they are underway. David's assignment is to make sure the iPad® with the needed charts is up and running. Soon after passing out through the gate in the sea wall, the waves become more boisterous and the wind increases. Jason predicts that they will have opportunity to test their sailing skills in heavy weather today.

With full sail, they begin making good speed and the wind-favored travel toward their destination. But the early strength of the wind suggests that an all-day outing may not have been the best choice. But, for now, they are having fun meeting the waves and feeling the boat heel (lean) as the wind pushes against the sails. The waves are a bit confused, first appearing to come from one direction, and then waves crossing from another.

"I'm glad you boys don't get seasick because it looks as if we could be in for a lively day," says Gramps. "For now, just enjoy the sailing. If you venture out on the foredeck you better plan on getting wet. Those waves are crashing into the bow pretty good every now and then. We even got some spray back here in the cockpit."

"Dave, remember how I showed you how to read the charts on the iPad®? As we leave the bay, I want you to monitor our course and watch to make sure we don't ground our boat on a sand bar or crash on underwater rocks. The chart gives you all that information and even shows us how deep the water is," says Gramps.

"Wow, these charts are pretty cool. They even show where our boat is on the map," Dave observes. "I bet Joseph would have liked to have had that kind of information."

"Yes," says Gramps. "When Joseph sailed his ships, he had some charts, but not a moving map to tell him where he was in the world. He had to determine that by taking calculations from the stars or being able to identify distant landmarks on the land. Many ships were wrecked by grounding on unseen obstacles, especially in the shoal-filled waters off Cape Cod and the islands. That's one of the reasons lighthouses were eventually deployed, so that ships could navigate by those land-based lights."

"There are many lighthouses. How did the captain know which lighthouse he was looking at," asks Sam.

"Great question," responds Gramps.

"Each lighthouse had a different light code. The code was sort of like Morse code, with light flashes. The frequency, sequence, and color of the blinks of the lighthouse let the captain know which lighthouse he was looking at," says Jason. "Sailing is mostly for recreation these days. A square-rigger is a tall sailing ship like the one Joseph sailed on commercially. Only a few museum ships of this kind exist today."

Jason continues, "I was overwhelmed with joy when I got a chance to help watch over the *Charles W. Morgan* at Mystic Harbor. I heard that it was the last of the American whaling fleet to survive. You might have noticed that she's over 106 feet long and has three masts."

Gramps continues the account, "That is a wooden-hull ship like Joseph's with three masts and rigging like whaling ships used for 200 years. Sailing that ship required a lot of ropes to set the sails and hold the masts, yards and deck gear. So 'learning the ropes' is a big part of the sailing process. Joseph's last command was the Empress with three masts and a crew of seven. By that time in his life, he had worked his way up from cabin boy to becoming captain and part owner of that ship. He was given full authority to buy and sell his cargo and even the ship itself, if he had a good offer."

"Dave, you get to man the tiller for the first part of our trip," says Gramps. "You remember how I taught you to keep the sail full of wind and what to do if the wind catches too much sail."

Dave says, "I think you said if the boat heels too much I need to turn the boat into the wind a bit. That will let more of the wind spill off the sail and we won't tip so far to the side. And if I turn too much upwind the sail will lose all the wind and will start flapping and making a crazy lot of noise."

"Good recall," says Gramps. "So, let's see how you do. When we sail 'close to the wind' like we are today it takes quite a bit of practice to keep from getting too much wind in the sail or not enough. You'll see how it works, right quick."

"Hey, thanks Gramps," says Dave. "This is kind-of fun. Except these waves seem to be going every which way today. Makes it hard to stay on course."

"This crazy wave pattern suggests that the wind is changing direction. We'll have to watch how fast this happens. Could be an indication of a storm later," replies Gramps. "Sometimes, the tides help make those crazy wave patterns, too."

"Jason, you manage the sails this trip. If the wind gets too strong, we may have to take in some sail or you may have to let the boom swing out a little more. We may have to roll up the jib (the front sail) some and maybe even reef the main sail. I think there is a good chance we may see some rough weather soon," says Gramps. Then to Sam he says, "Feel free to practice the knots Jason taught you while we sail today. Since our sailboat doesn't travel all that fast there should be plenty of time to learn some new ones too. We don't have as many ropes on this boat as the one Jason told us about, but the cables and ropes here are still important to the health of the boat and the effectiveness of the sail."

After sailing for an hour or so longer, Gramps notices that the wind is shifting rather significantly and increasing in strength, something that Buzzards Bay is famous for. He announces that they would be returning home. "I'm afraid, by the looks of things, that we may already have some trouble returning to port. The wind is now almost dead against us as we head home. That means it will take much longer to get back than it has taken us to get to where we are now. All right crew, prepare to tack to Starboard. We'll have to be snappy or we won't be able to bring her full around." Each person performs their role well as they had practiced on an earlier voyage. They then settle in for a wild ride. The waves are now regularly breaking over the bow and the boat is bobbing vigorously.

Gramps checks to see if each boy has on his life jacket and cautions them to be very careful as they move around the boat. "If you go forward you will want to clip on a security line. David, help roll up the jib [that's the sail in front of the mast]. We don't need that much sail up with this wind."

Just then a blast of wind and a wave at the same time tip the boat way over, making the occupants of the cockpit end up in a pile on the low side. They hear crashing sounds in the cabin as well, as many items slide off the stove and fall off the shelves. But, as designed, the boat soon rights itself and everyone is able to sort themselves out to their previous positions.

For sure it is time to take in some sail. Just as David releases the sheet (the rope holding the jib) Gramps notices that the knot at the end of the rope has come out, but it is too late! As Sam releases the rope, it jumps off the winch and yanks out of his grasp. The jib goes sailing wildly out of control, and the rope that should have held it is now thrashing like a whip from the uncontrolled sail, sometimes trailing in the water, and then again snapping back threateningly at the passengers. All at once, the mad rope snaps skyward, wrapping itself around the mast, and tangling itself near the spreader about half way up the mast. No longer thrashing around, the rope is now captive, but the jib remains out of control and cannot be furled. This is a predicament Gramps has never encountered before! The knotted rope prevents lowering the main sail as well. With the wind as fierce as it is, Gramps makes a decision to "run with the wind," meaning they would go with the wind rather than against it. That would send them in the opposite direction from home, but would ease the force of the wind in the sails. It also means they would be bounding over the waves with even greater speed. The boat becomes difficult to manage and is nearly out of control. The untrimmed sails are creating a fearful racket, thrashing wildly.

Now is the time to get creative. Perhaps those knots Sam has been learning will come to good use now, but how? Someone will have to go up the mast and untangle the renegade rope or the sails will tear themselves to pieces. With the ship rocking wildly, it will be a risky maneuver. Gramps couldn't imagine himself up on that mast swinging out over the water one way and then the other. Sam offers to try to go up the mast, but Gramps discourages him. "You could easily fall overboard and a rescue in these conditions would be difficult." Gramps is careful to remind them how to use the tethered life-sling in case someone does fall overboard. Looking up the mast, Gramps suggests, "We could help pull you up with the spare halyard, but you would need a way to help pull yourself up too."

Then Sam remembers a knot he had learned that could be used as an ascender. He tells Gramps about it but Gramps is skeptical. "You'd need to be able to move it up as you go," he responds.

"That's just what this knot is good for," Sam replies. "You put your foot in this loop and as you step up with one foot, you move the loop for the other foot higher."

It is hard to hear above the noise of the waves and the flapping of the sail.

"Well," Gramps says, "I guess you can try it down low and if it works you can go higher. Here, take this halyard and tie it around your waist with a good bowline knot. We will belay you with the halyard over the winch. Be careful. Hang on tight."

> *Sam makes some adjustments with his knot and soon finds he can climb one step at a time right up the mast using his ascender knot, one for each foot. It looks easy enough, but on the gyrating mast Sam knows he could easily fall overboard.*

Sam makes some adjustments with his knot and soon finds he can climb one step at a time right up the mast using his ascender knot, one for each foot. It looks easy enough, but on the gyrating mast Sam knows he could easily fall overboard. At about twenty feet up the mast, the boat beneath him looks much smaller than it had on deck. The thrashing sail threatens to knock loose his grip. He is almost to the spreader now where the tangled rope had lodged itself. With care, Sam tries to unravel the knotted rope, being careful not to let his fingers get caught under the rope as it is jerked this way and that. Finally, he is able to loosen the knotted rope. He knows he needs to be careful not to let it go again as he descends. He tries holding the tugging rope in his teeth to leave both hands free to hold on to the mast, but the rope jerks so wildly he is afraid it will yank his teeth out. So, he makes the best of it by gripping the rope in the same hand that he holds on to the mast with. The descent is a little easier than the way up because he can just slide down with his speed controlled by the halyard that Gramps is paying out over the winch as he comes down. The whole crew cooperates in keeping the boat flying downwind and trying to minimize the impact of the waves on the rocking boat and the swaying mast. At last, Sam is on deck again and hands the errant rope to Gramps who quickly wraps it around the winch where it should have been. He firmly ties a knot in the end of it that will prevent it from making another escape. Sam, still shaking with fatigue and fear, slumps onto the bench in the cockpit to recover his nerves.

Gramps gives instructions for turning the boat toward home. With the flapping sails now tamed, it is considerably quieter, but the boat still pounds through the waves. It takes some time to recover the distance they had lost heading in the wrong direction, but now, with the boat once again under control, everyone is grateful to see the harbor come into view. As they pass through the seawall gate, the waves are suddenly subdued and the wind blocked by surrounding buildings and trees, taking on a more docile attitude.

In the few minutes it takes to reach their mooring, Gramps recounts a couple of Joseph's near fatal experiences at sea. The first story he tells was how Joseph, just fifteen years old, was asked to climb the mast to see if there were any other ships that could be seen nearby. As he was descending, he lost his grip and fell backward toward the ship's deck below. On the way down, he hit another rope that bounced him over the side of the ship. As Joseph surfaced from his plunge into the ocean, he saw that the ship was swiftly passing away from him. One of the sailors hurled a rope with all his might, and Joseph was just able to catch the end of it. Hanging on with all his strength the other sailors were able to pull him back to the ship. Only when he was standing dripping on the deck did the sailors think to ask about the shark that had trailed their ship for hours, never leaving its position behind the ship. At the mention of the shark, Joseph began shaking with fear and weakness. The shark was found peacefully swimming on the opposite side of the ship from where Joseph had fallen in. What made the shark change its position just when Joseph fell into the water? Could there be a God who was protecting him? Joseph pondered what appeared to be providential intervention to save his life.

Nearing their mooring now Dave asks if he could be the first to tell the girls about today's adventure. Jason says he would add details Dave forgot. Sam wants to tell what it was like up on the mast. Gramps thinks about all the trouble that a missing knot had caused and how the right knot had helped to save their lives.

"I wonder if the girls will wish they had been along with us?" Jason asks.

"They could be mighty glad they had stayed home," Dave adds.

Sam says, "They'll probably have their own story to tell about the tour they gave today."

"Well," says Gramps, "I think we will have plenty to share tonight, but right now, let's get hooked up to our mooring and tidy up the boat before we get in the dinghy. We need to leave things in 'ship shape' you know."

What fun they have that evening as they all share their stories over a light supper of fruit, nuts, popcorn, and hot chocolate. They also have a thankful prayer meeting, grateful they are all together again.

After the guys finish telling their sailing adventures for the day, Gramma remarks, "We had our own little miracle of 'God will provide.' Our tour group turned out to be a mixture of a Portuguese family reunion and friends, all with limited English speaking skills. First, I tried my limited Spanish vocabulary, but that didn't do it. The group's leaders let me know that maybe they would just look around and be happy with that, but I could see the sadness and near tears in the older ladies' eyes, and knew that wasn't enough. Silently, I was praying for help."

"You will never guess who come to our rescue—Patsy!" Mae Lee adds with a giggle.

"Patsy said that she felt impressed to come back even though she hadn't planned to, couldn't get out of her mind," Gramma continues.

Gramps questions, "How could our 'Bawstin' accented friend help with that?"

Answering, Gramma says, "I knew you wouldn't believe it, I didn't at first, but she grew up in a Portuguese speaking neighborhood and learned the language as a child. After the tour, she told me more of the history of this area.

"At one time New Bedford was known as the 'Portuguese capital of the United States.' At the beginning of the nineteenth century the whaling industry shifted from Newport, Rhode Island, to New Bedford, which then became the town with the largest number of Portuguese, actually sixteen percent of the city's entire population. I could tell that Patsy really connected with the group and they were so appreciative. When the tour was over, Patsy had to get back to the animal shelter right away, but remarked that she was glad she had come because now she had learned more about this museum, Joseph Bates' life, and his Biblical understanding."

Mae Lee adds, "Patsy said that when she got home this evening, she was going to find her Bible and start reading it more!"

"God still does provide," Gramps responds, "our extremity is truly God's opportunity!"

Eventually, the warmth of the fireplace and the fatigue from the day's adventures act as a sedative, sending everyone to their places of slumber earlier than usual. "I'll take you to the small apartment by the museum, Jason. Then tomorrow, when we get back from the airport, I'll give you a tour, if you'd like that," Gramps offers.

"I was hoping that would happen. It will make my day off most enjoyable. This has been a high day for me. I'm so happy that Sam has you for a role model in this life. God is good," Jason finishes.

Gramps adds, "All the time!"

CHAPTER THIRTEEN

THE LAST DAY of the grandchildren's visit arrives almost unexpectedly. Everyone knew it would come, but now that it is here, it is an unwanted ending. So many good times were squeezed into the past ten days! These memories echo and re-echo through Dave's thinking, awakening him in the early morning hours, and keeping him awake. They create all kinds of questions about his future. He decides that Gramps might be able to help. Getting out of bed and leaving the room quietly enough so that even Sam didn't hear him, he tiptoes down to the living room. Sure enough, Gramps is awake, too, reading his Bible.

Stopping in the shadows of the early morning light filtering through the lace curtains, Dave stands motionless, wanting to memorize this setting. How much this has come to mean to him. Would he ever experience this again? Would he be able to tuck it into some corner of his memory and find it when he needed it?

"Gramps," Dave whispers, startling him.

Looking up from his reading, surprised, but pleased, Gramps responds, "I'm glad you've come to join me. Here, have a seat."

Dave starts, "I've got questions. Do you think that when Bates was fourteen, he was prepared for all that he was going to do and knew how to do it? How did he survive all his mishaps?"

After thinking a little while, Gramps asks, "What do you think?"

Dave suggests, "God must have directed him, at least some of the time, when Bates listened to Him. That's the problem, how do I know when it's God speaking to me and not just my own imagination?"

"The way I understand it," Gramps explains, "God promises to speak to us when we ask Him. However, we have to ask without telling Him what we want to hear. That's not always easy, but it's possible. We have the promised gift of the Holy Spirit when we desire it with our whole being and are willing to put our own selfish interests aside. It's the same Holy Spirit, who inspired your parents to adventure for God into doing their mission trip. When we fully give ourselves to the Lord, He provides the wind for our sails and charts our course."

Dave adds, "I know that Bates would have liked that thought, and maybe added to it these words, 'Though, there be troubled waters, in God we have a lighthouse that directs us to a safe harbor, because He is the Pilot for our trip of life and an anchor to our souls.'"

"Well said, Mate! It sounds like you're ready to set sail in life's journey," observes Gramps. "Why don't we seal it with prayer? Dear God of our present and future, we place ourselves into Your hands. Help us to turn to You with every decision we need to make. Putting self aside is not easy and impossible without You. We ask for this miracle, praying for forgiveness for our past mistakes and strength for today. In Christ's name, we pray. Amen."

> « That's the problem, how do I know when it's God speaking to me and not just my own imagination? »

The quietness of the morning is suddenly broken by voices from upstairs and the sound of running feet. Packing for the day's journey needs completion. Dave gives Gramps a hug and runs upstairs to join in the task. Gramma dashes downstairs and rushes straight to the kitchen. Time is of the essence!

After a healthy, hearty breakfast, packed luggage set by the door, a song of praise, and a prayer for protection, the family heads out to the car just in time to see a whole retinue of friends arrive to say good-bye. Jason, Auntie Mabel with Lucy, and Patsy surround them with sad words of parting. Jason says, with tears in his eyes, "Sammy, how can I leave you another time? You will write to me, send me pictures of yourself to my cell phone, and come back to visit if you can?"

Sam replies, "Of course I will, you were like a dad to me when I had none. You can come visit me, too. I'm sure my parents won't mind. You have my address and phone number. We won't lose each

other again, I promise." Afraid he will break into tears, Sam turns away, pushes his luggage into Gramps' truck and jumps into the back seat, loudly calling out, "First one in and ready to leave!"

Mae Lee picks up Lucy, snuggles her close and kisses her on the top of her head. Then she turns and gives Auntie Mabel a lasting hug. At first, Mabel doesn't know how to react to this hug, she just stands like a statue, finally her arms slowly come down and surround Mae Lee with a returning embrace. Patsy, seeing this, nudges Gramma, and points it out with a smile, and whispers, "Love can melt hearts of steel." When

Mae Lee breaks away, Patsy calls out, "Hey, kid, you ain't goin' away without sharing a hug with me, too, are ya?"

Mae Lee responds, "Of course not, I'm going to be missing you a lot. Thank you again for Lucy, you'll have to come see her and Auntie Mabel sometimes while I'm gone. Give them each a hug from me."

While hugging Mae Lee, Patsy responds, "Lucy will put up with a hug from me and that's about far as it goes, I'm sure. Take care and do come back."

At this point, Gramps calls out, "Everyone in the truck that's going to the airport. I see Sam is already there, hurry." As Gramps turns to get in, Jason comes over to the driver's side of the truck to ask some directions. While they're talking, Gramps doesn't see or hear what is happening in the back seat. Dave gets in one side, but as Mae Lee is going to get in on the other side, she stops with a look of horror. "I don't have Bagel!"

"Where is he?" Sam asks.

Mae Lee answers, "I don't know for sure!"

"Okay, I'll go back and get him, I'm quicker than you," with that Sam jumps out and sprints back into the house. Mae Lee climbs into the middle of the backseat to wait. Gramma, not hearing about or seeing Mae Lee's dilemma because she is talking with Patsy, turns, shuts both the backseat doors and her own after she is seated. Gramps, noticing the lateness of the hour and that Gramma is inside, quickly starts the engine, turns the truck, waves one last time and speeds off.

At this turn of events, Mae Lee and Dave first stare at each other and try to get the attention of their grandparents. Gramps says, "We can't talk now, I've got to concentrate on my driving and Gramma has to find the directions on her phone's GPS because we get lost every time we try to find that obscure airport. Hope we make it on time. It's going to be close!" Repeatedly the kids try to tell their grandparents that Sam is not with them, but get hushed each time.

Meanwhile, Sam finally comes running out of the house, just to see their vehicle disappear around the corner. "Maybe if I run, I can catch them at the light," Sam says aloud.

Jason responds, "Don't try, Mabel saw what happened and almost ran to her garage to get her car, I guess. Here she comes now. Wow! I haven't seen a 1969 American Rambler in a long time. I'm pretty sure that's what it is. Well, God speed, Sammy. I'm praying you'll make it in time."

When Mabel's car gets beside him, she yells, "Jump in the back seat and hang on." After Sam complies, Mabel's car shoots down the drive with gravel spitting out behind them. "Can you tell me the way to go to the airport, Sam?" she yells over her shoulder.

"I think I remember the way, I'm usually pretty good with directions," Sam calls back, hanging onto a door support as they zoom around a curve.

After the Rambler speeds through two yellow, almost red, lights, Sam thinks about what he should do to help in this situation. Grabbing his cell phone, he calls Dave, "Hey, don't worry about me, tell Gramps that Mabel got out her car and we will meet you at the airport!"

"Wow!" Dave responds, "I didn't even know she had one!"

On hearing Dave's phone ring, Gramma asks, "Who was that?"

"Oh, it was just Sam," Dave answers casually.

"What?" Gramma says, finally looking into the back seat, "Why didn't you tell us?"

"We tried, but you wouldn't listen!" Gramps quickly starts putting his brakes on to turn around. "No, you don't need to go back. Mabel has him in her car and will meet us at the airport."

"This will be interesting!" Gramps responds, as he resumes their speed.

Mabel, concentrating on her driving, yet wanting to say something to Sam before she loses him as a passenger, finally manages to get it said, "I'm sorry, Sam, that I didn't always speak nicely to you. You're really a kindhearted, giving, caring person. I misjudged you. Because I've had bad experiences with some of the town boys from New Bedford, I made the mistake of treating you all the same because of my fears. It's not an excuse for my wrongdoing, but it's the reason for it. Will you forgive me?"

Sam, while somewhat distracted by Mabel's precarious speed driver skills, manages to respond with, "Not to worry, it's okay. We're friends now. That's all that matters. I really appreciate you doing this."

While they are rounding the last bend in the airport's entryway, Sam notices that Mabel is passing Gramps's truck without recognizing it. Quietly laughing to himself, Sam says, "Yes! Beat 'em there! Auntie Mabel, great job!" When the Rambler screeches to a halt, Sam jumps out and runs to where Gramps' truck is parked to get his luggage, singing out, "I got here before you did, nah, nah, nah! What a ride!"

With the whole family helping, they get into the airport lobby just in time to check the grandchildren in before it is too late. After quick hugs and kisses, the passengers half run down the ramp to the tarmac and board the plane, waving as they go. Once the plane lifts off, Gramma practically collapses against Gramps, who sums up the whole ordeal with his usual, "At least it's a sunny day with a light breeze."

We invite you to view the complete
selection of titles we publish at:
www.TEACHServices.com

We encourage you to write us
with your thoughts about this,
or any other book we publish at:
info@TEACHServices.com

TEACH Services' titles may be purchased in
bulk quantities for educational, fund-raising,
business, or promotional use.
bulksales@TEACHServices.com

Finally, if you are interested in seeing
your own book in print, please contact us at:
publishing@TEACHServices.com

We are happy to review your manuscript at no charge.

www.ingramcontent.com/pod-product-compliance
Lightning Source LLC
Chambersburg PA
CBHW040313170426
43195CB00020B/2956